TRADITIONAL IRONWORK DESIGNS

Josef Feller

DOVER PUBLICATIONS, INC.
Mineola, New York

Note

Over the centuries, ironwork in Europe gradually evolved to levels of great beauty and usefulness as artists and artisans lavished a high degree of creativity and craftsmanship on the production of even the most mundane items. By the second half of the nineteenth century, moreover, new industrial techniques had allowed the mass production of structural and ornamental ironwork in a proliferation of styles, from the elegantly simple to elaborate and ornate.

In this invaluable design resource you'll find over 270 carefully selected illustrations from a classic three-volume German portfolio published just before the turn of the twentieth century. Included are highly decorative designs for gates, railings, window grilles, brackets, light and flower stands, weather vanes, andirons, commercial signs, canopies, verandas, and many more.

Architects, preservationists, antique dealers, decorators, and collectors will find this profusely illustrated volume a rich and absorbing reprise of a host of ironwork designs available in the late nineteenth century for use in architectural design and interior decoration of both private and public buildings. Artists, designers and craftspeople will discover in these designs not only an immediate source of usable permission-free motifs, but an ongoing fount of artistic and craft inspiration.

Bibliographical Note

Traditional Ironwork Designs is a new selection of plates reproduced from *Die Schmiedekunst: zum praktischen Gebrauche für Schlosser und Schmiede*, originally published in three volumes by F. Wolfrum, Dusseldorf, 1892–1899?

DOVER *Pictorial Archive* SERIES

International Standard Book Number: 0-486-44362-0

Manufactured in the United States of America
Dover Publications, Inc., 31 East 2nd Street, Mineola, N.Y. 11501

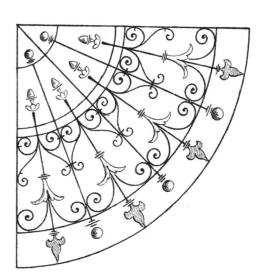

10   Flat Iron, Round Iron

16 Flat Iron, Round Iron

18 Round Iron

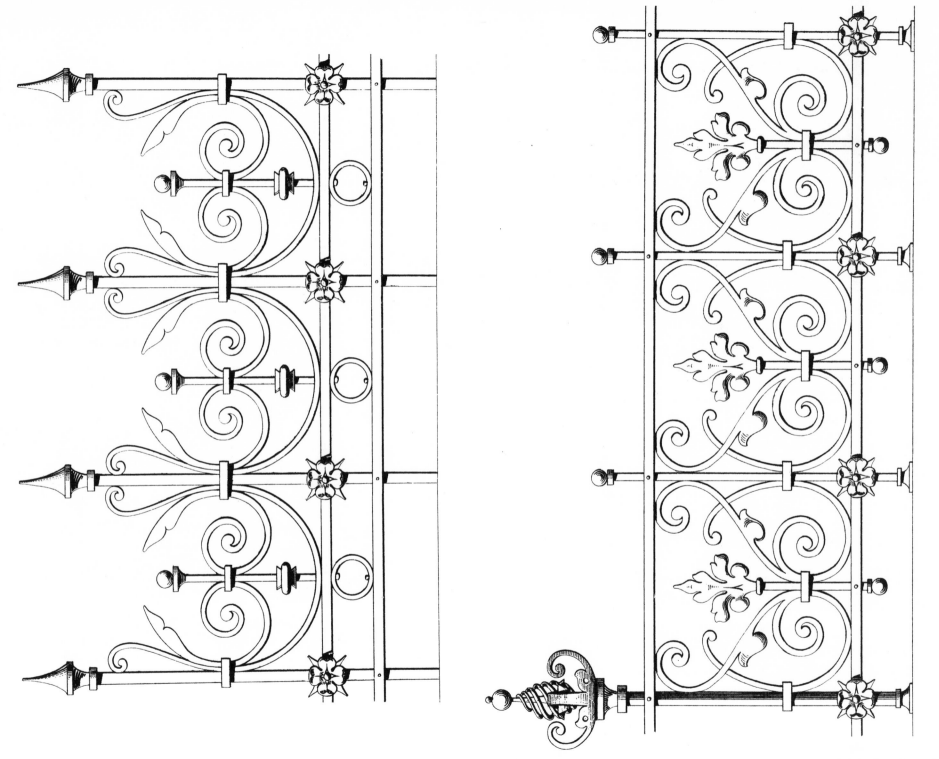

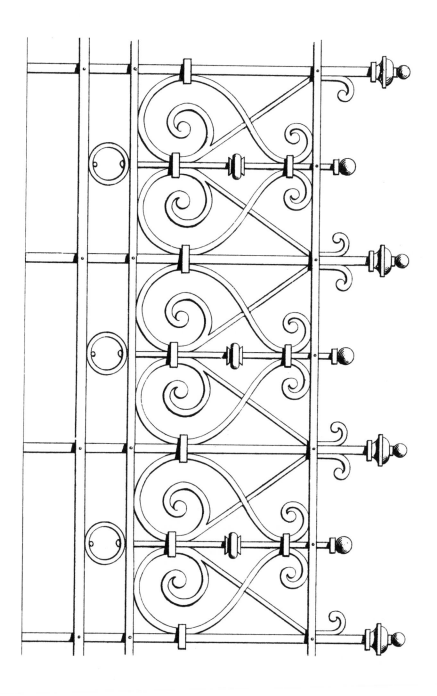

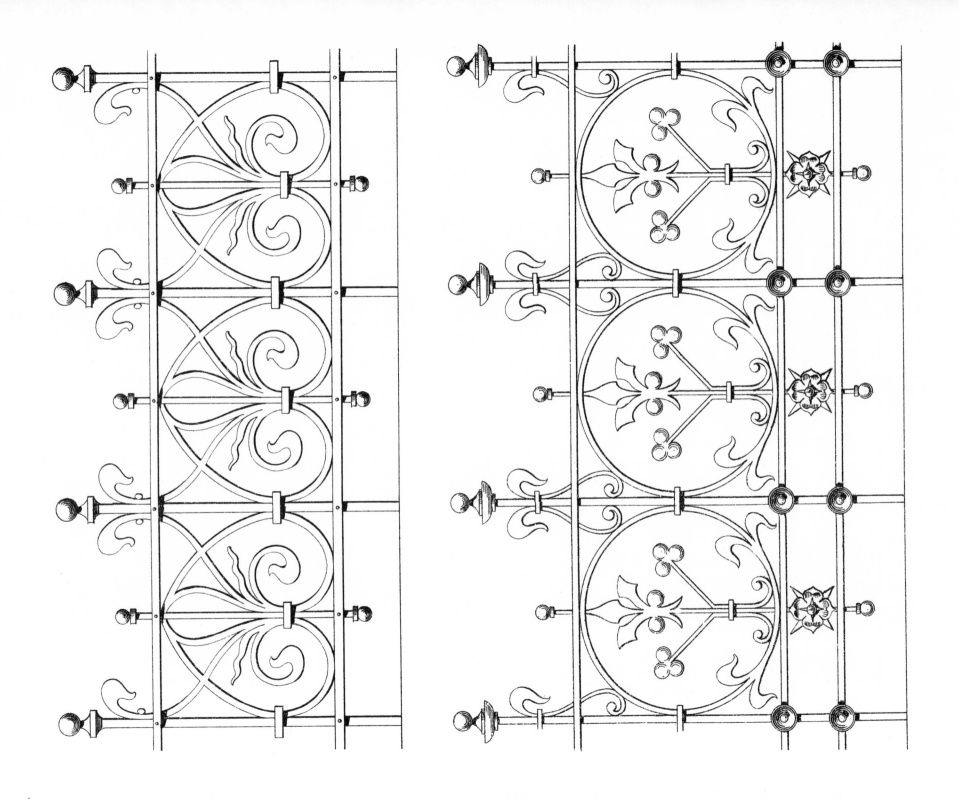

22   Ridge or roof railings

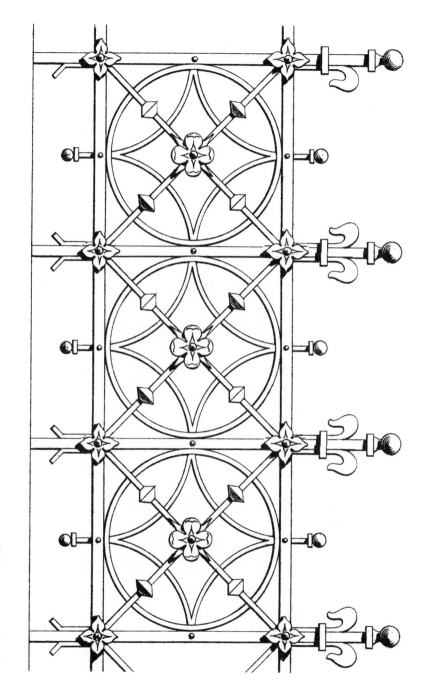

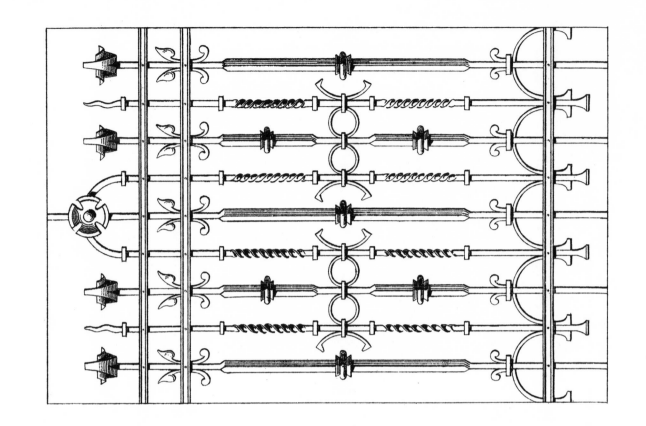

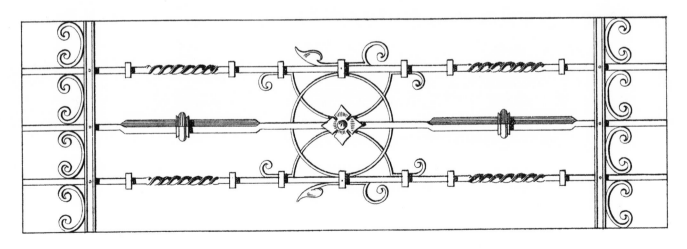

24   Window balustrade, grilles

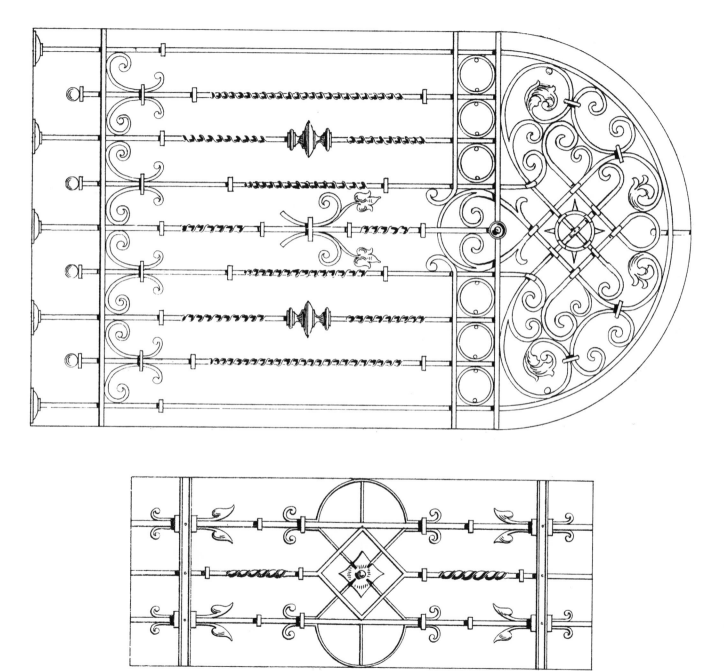

26   Window balustrades, grille

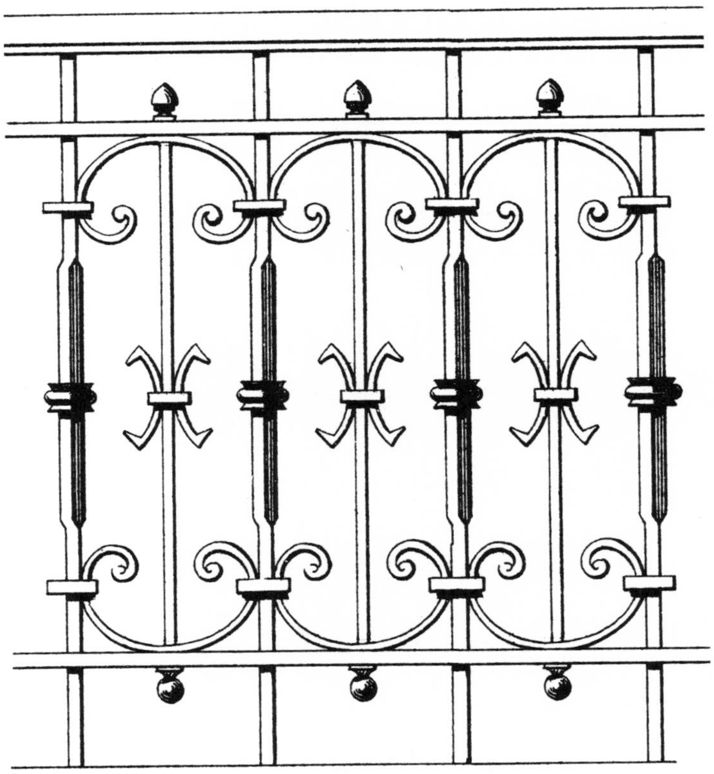

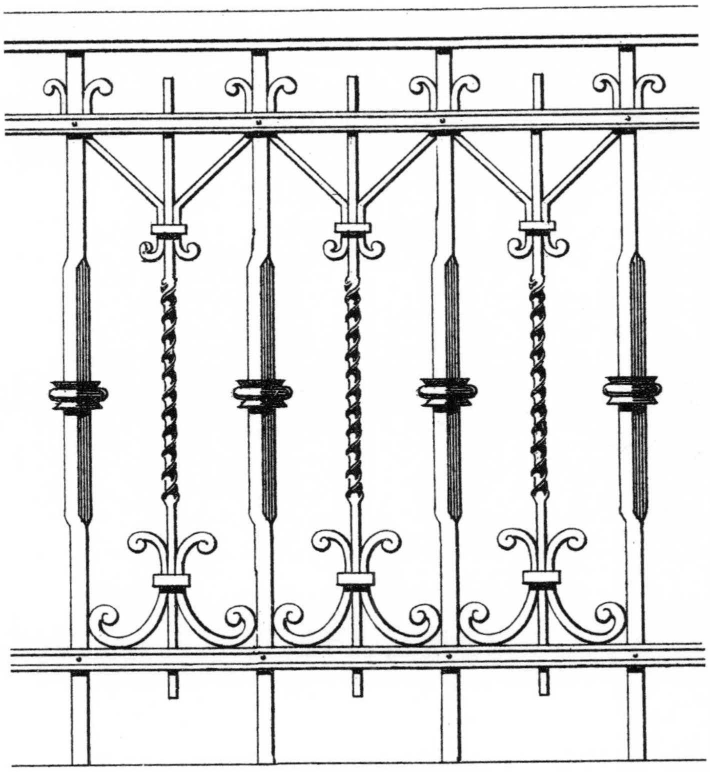

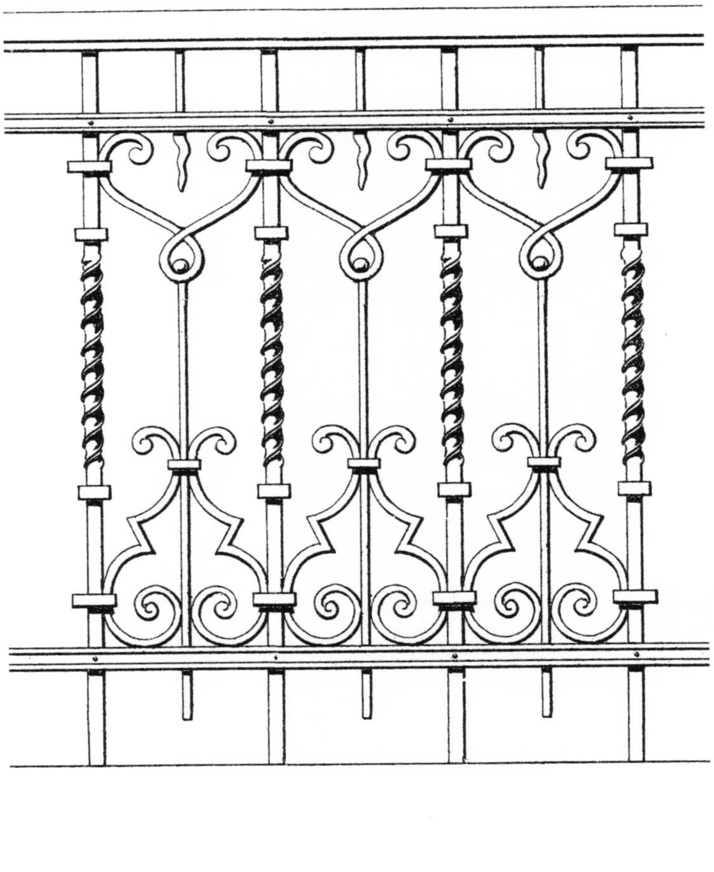

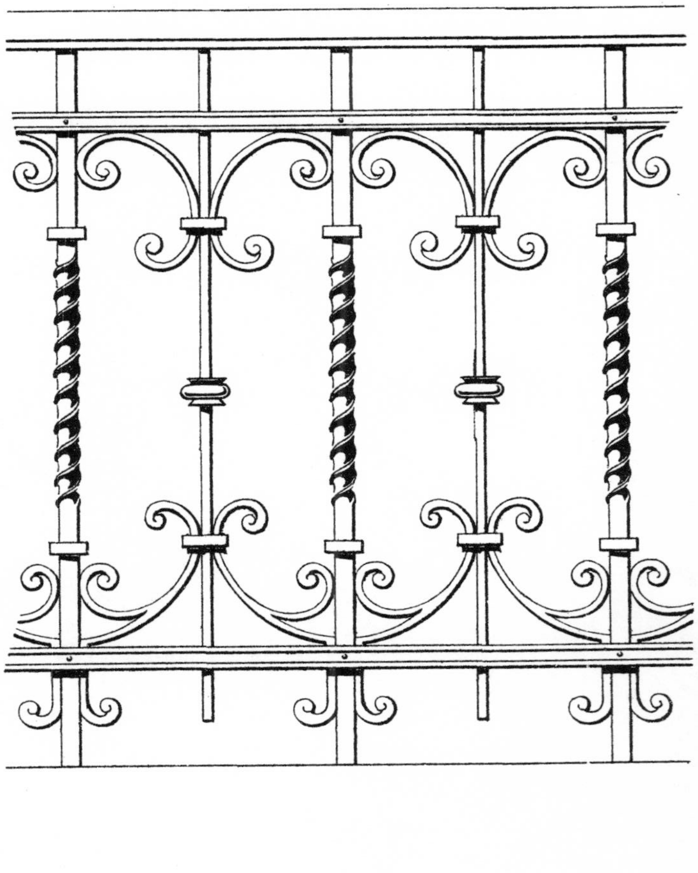

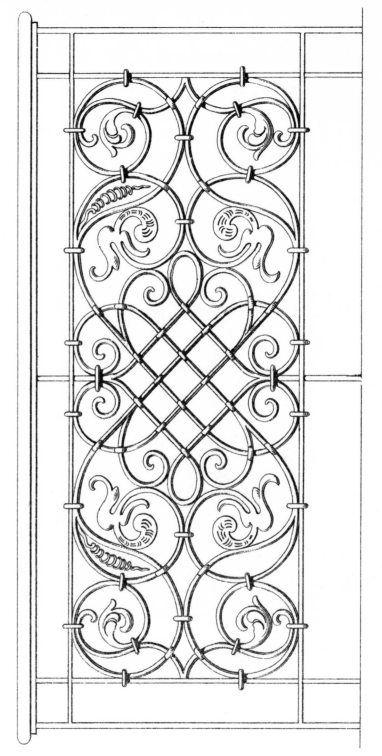

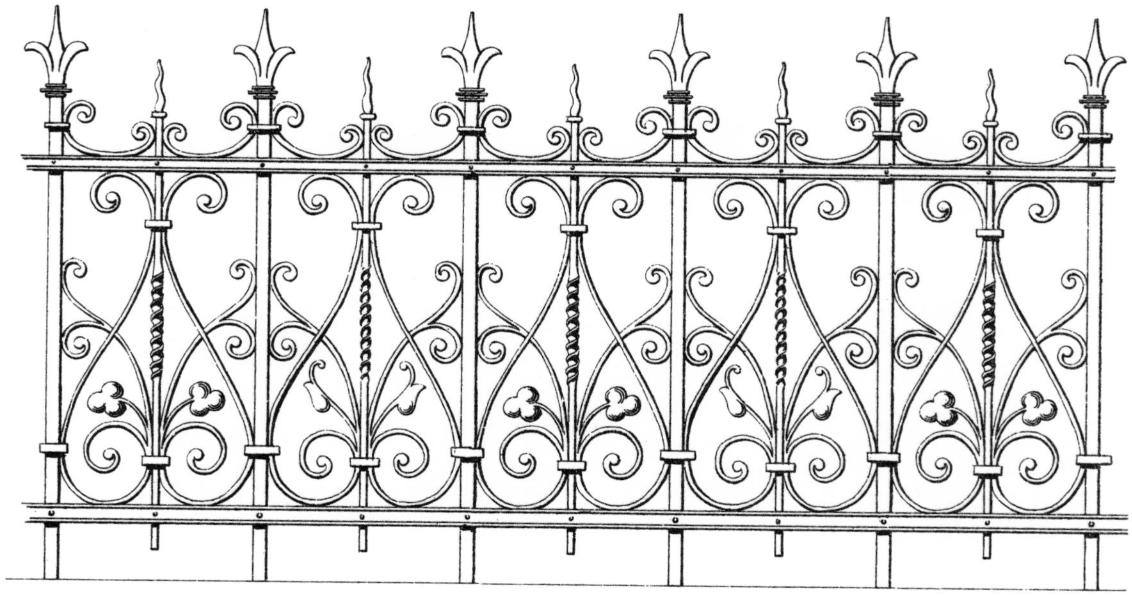

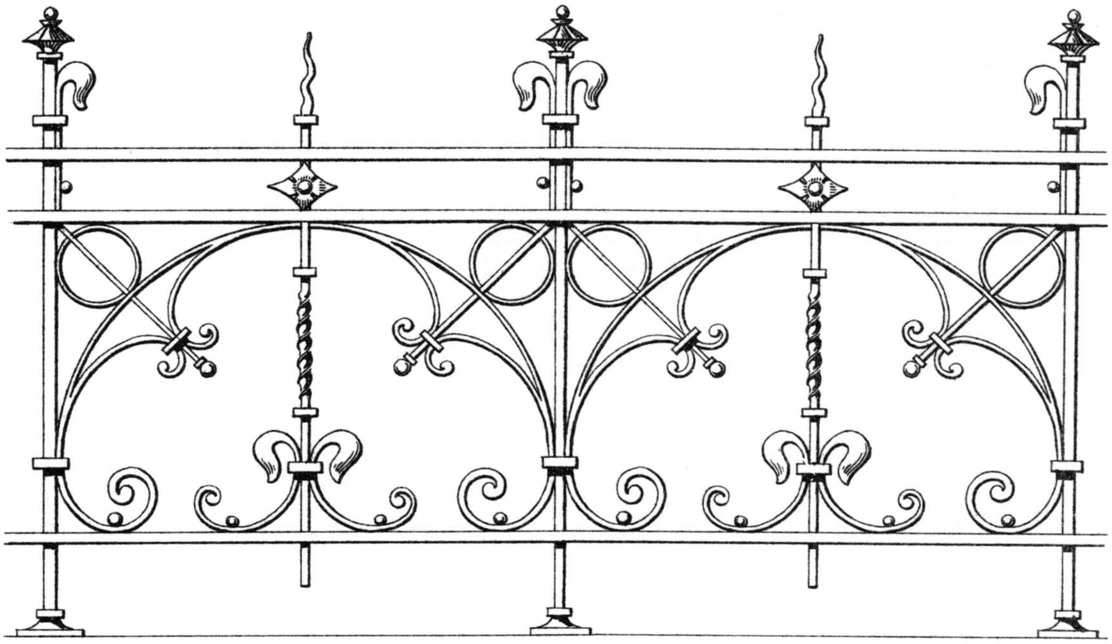

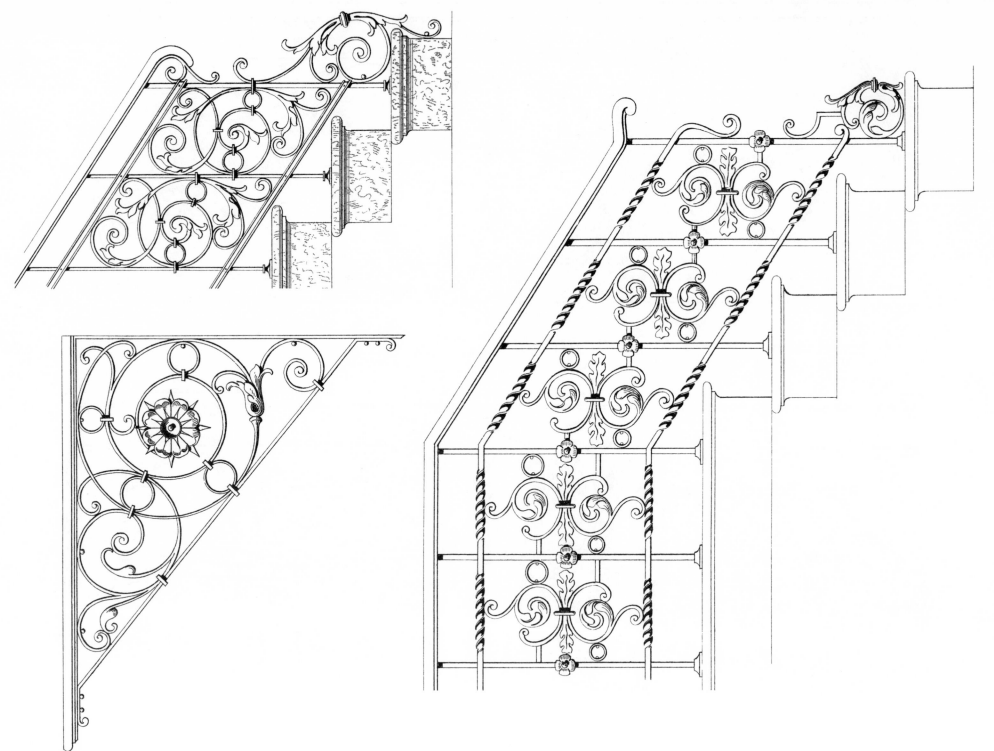

36   Bracket, stair railings

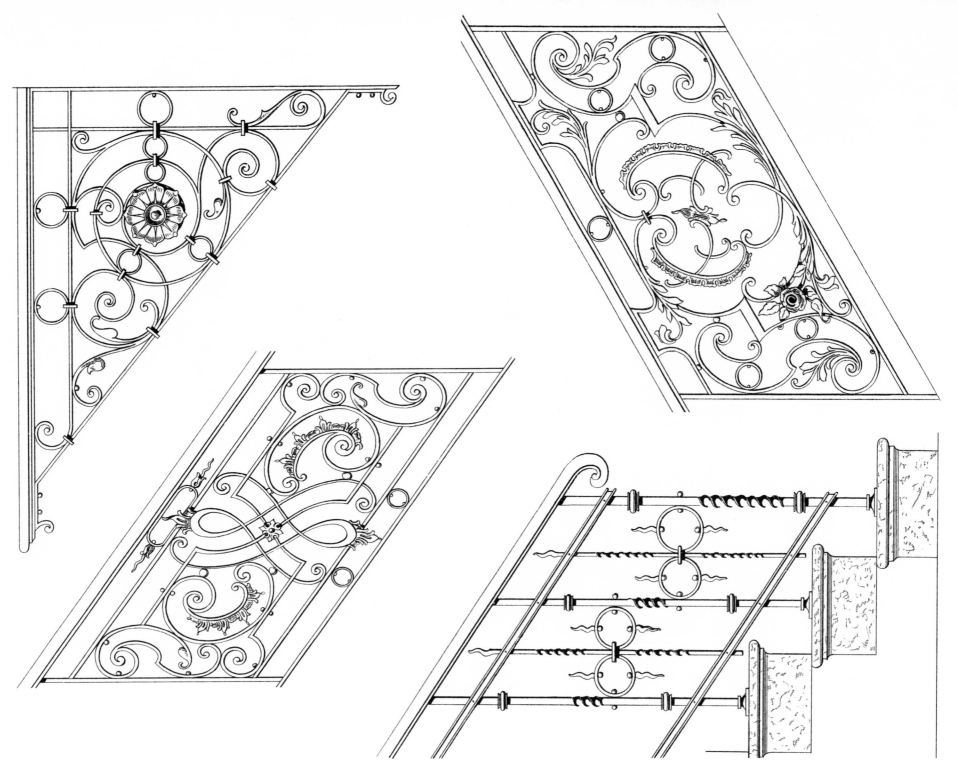

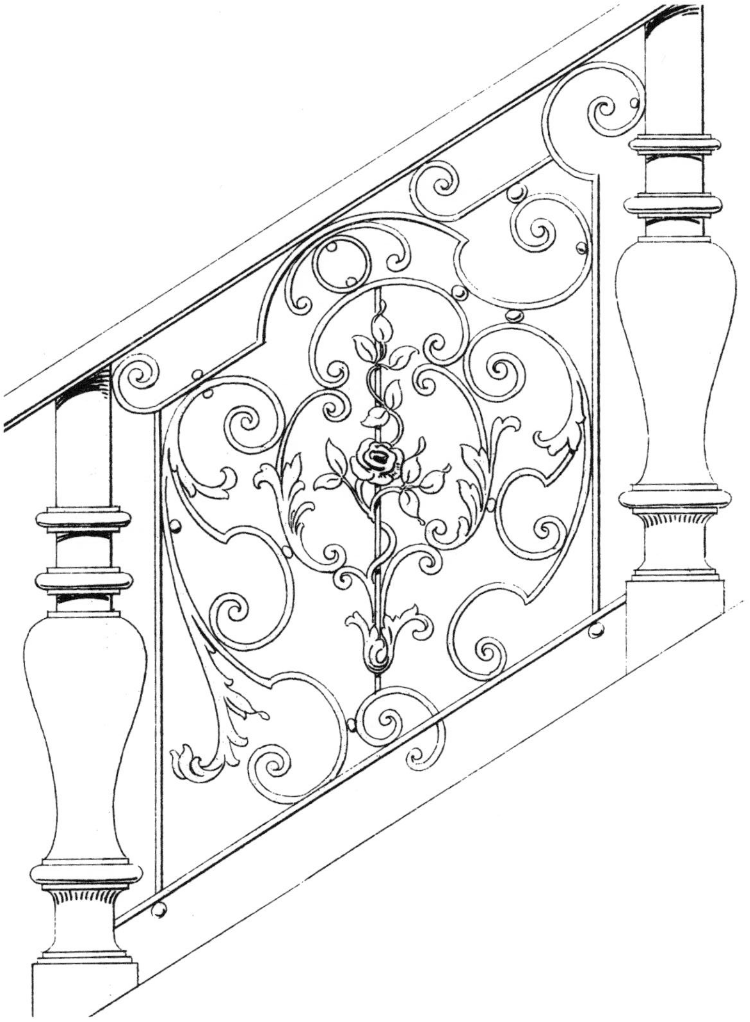

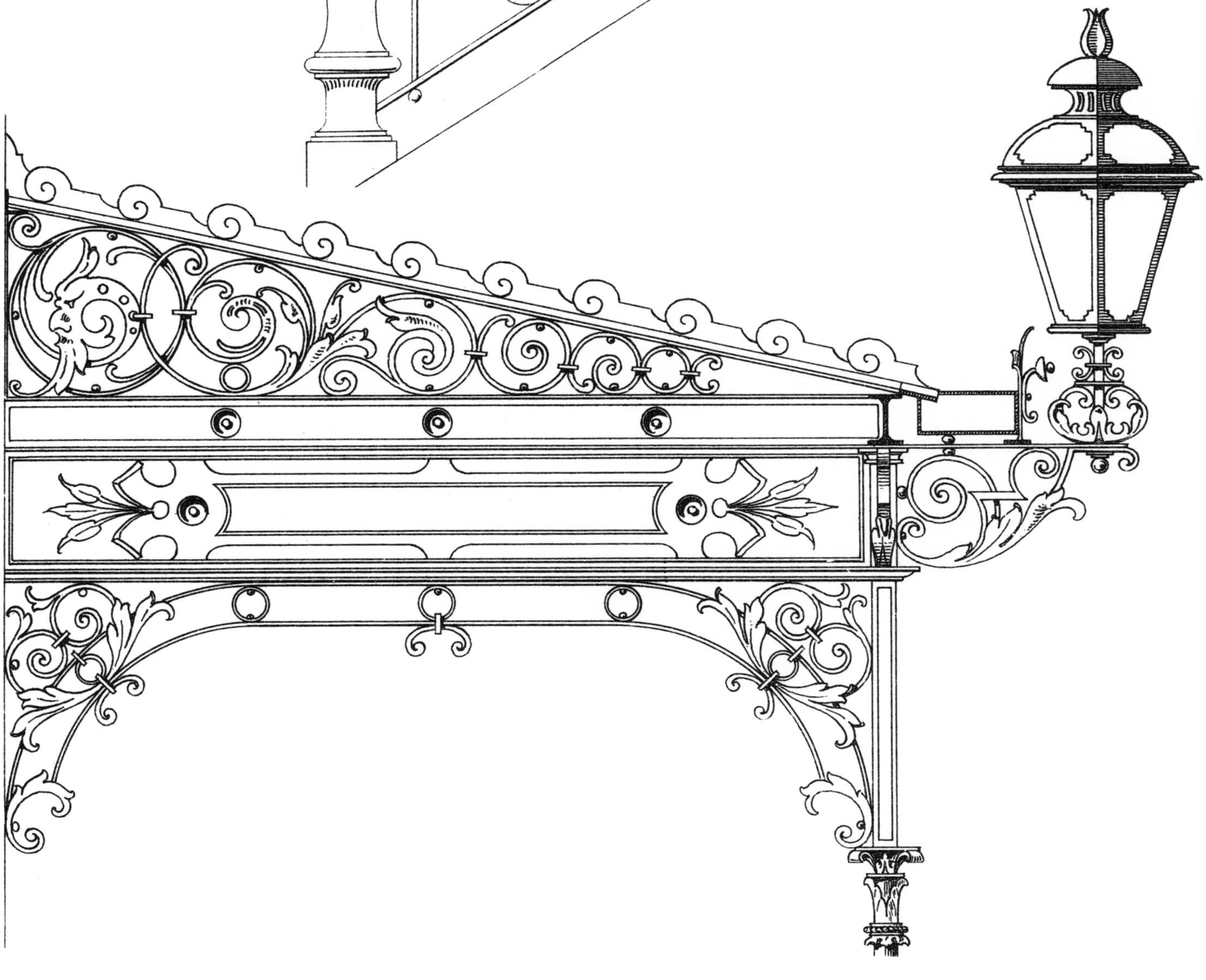

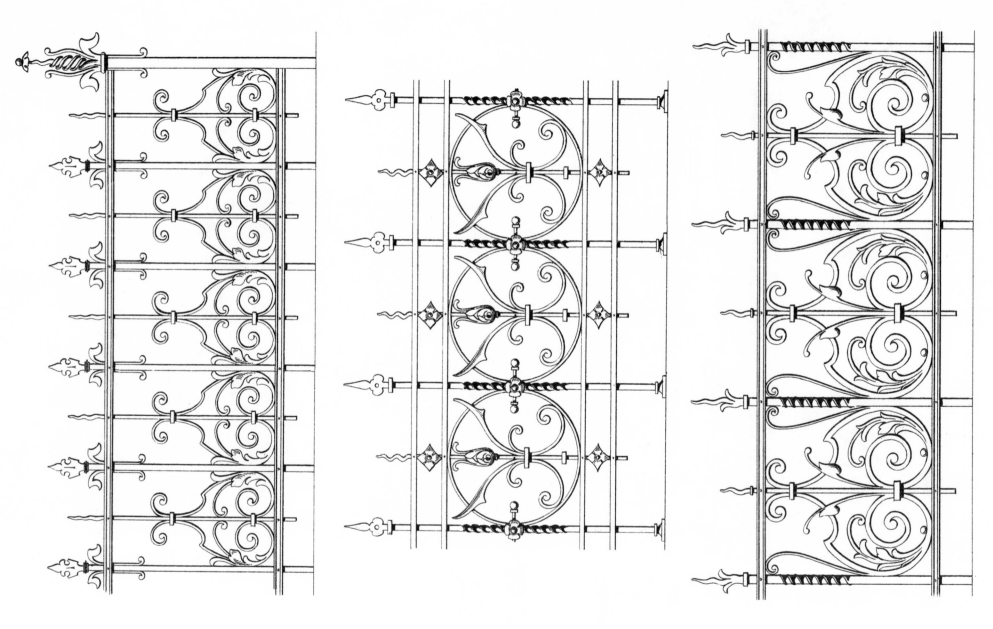

40 Grave railings

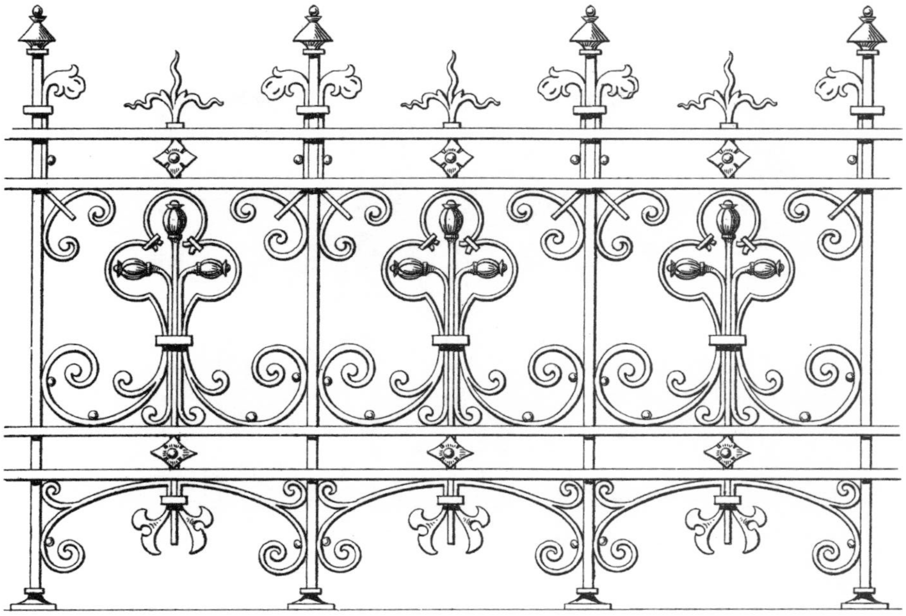

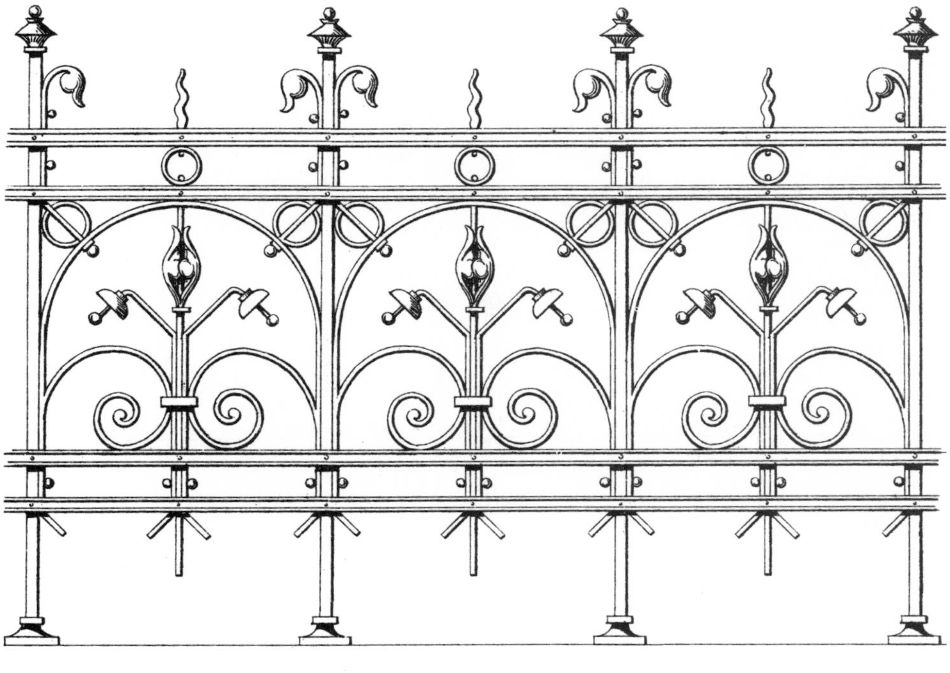

42   Grave railings

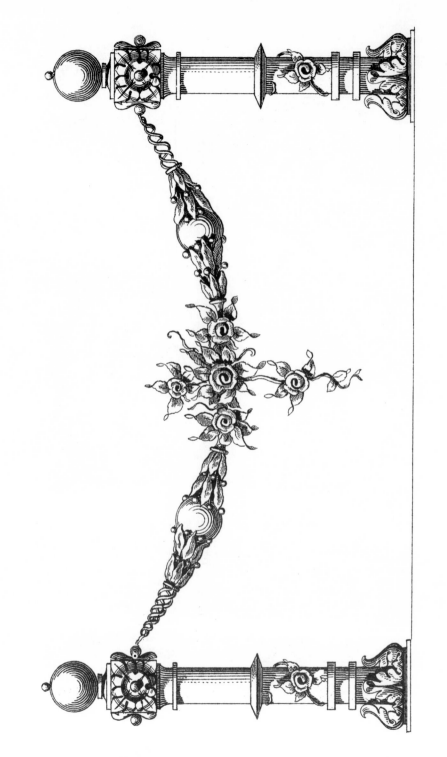

44 Grave railings

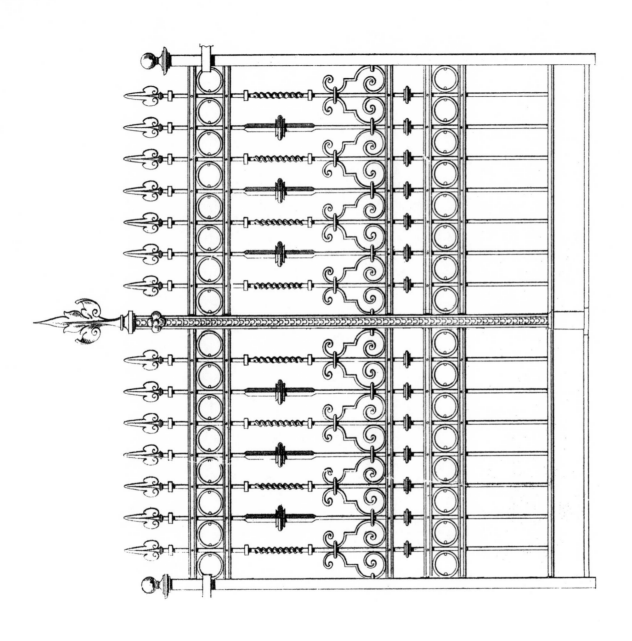

46 Gate, grave railing

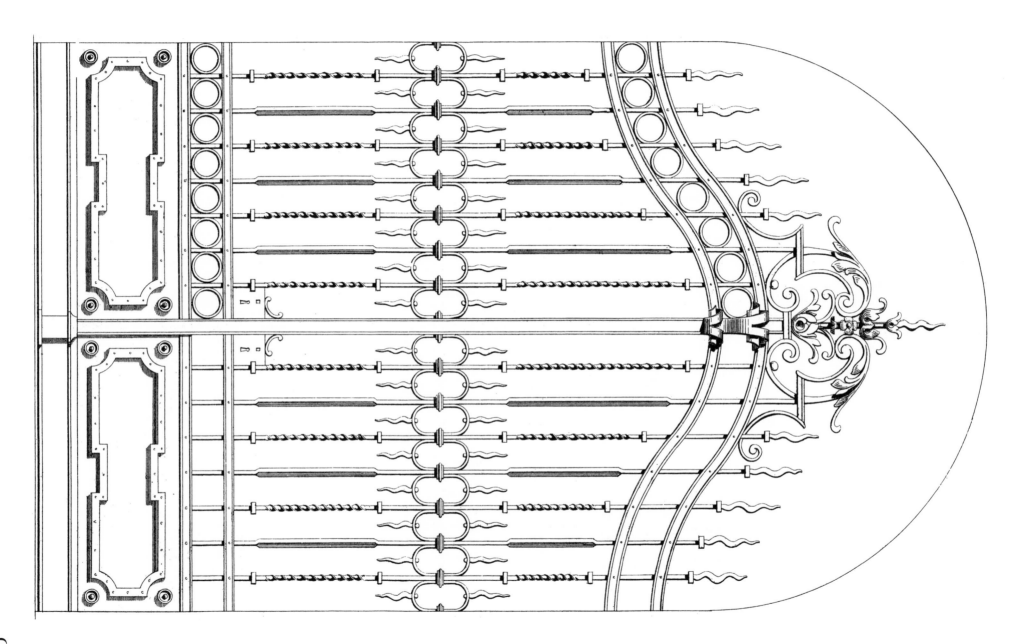

48 Grave railing, gate

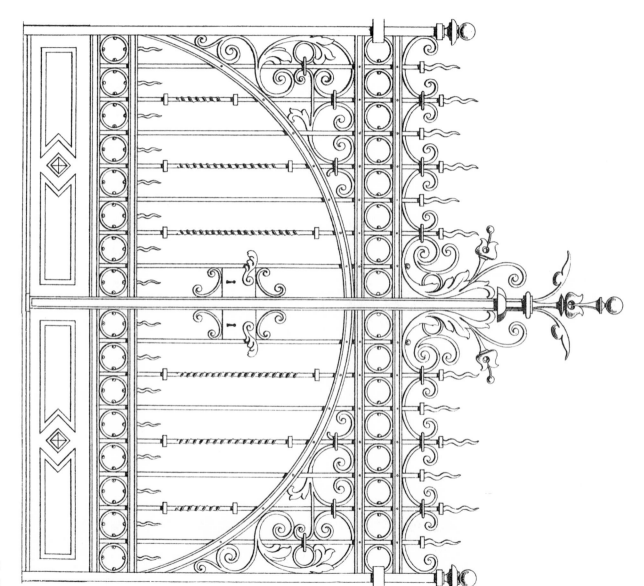
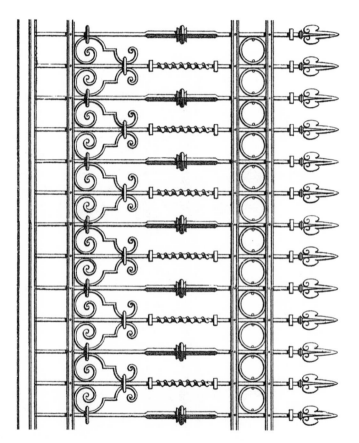

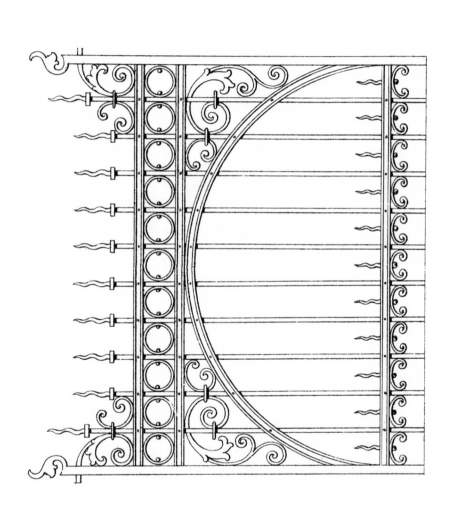

52 Gate

Gate 53

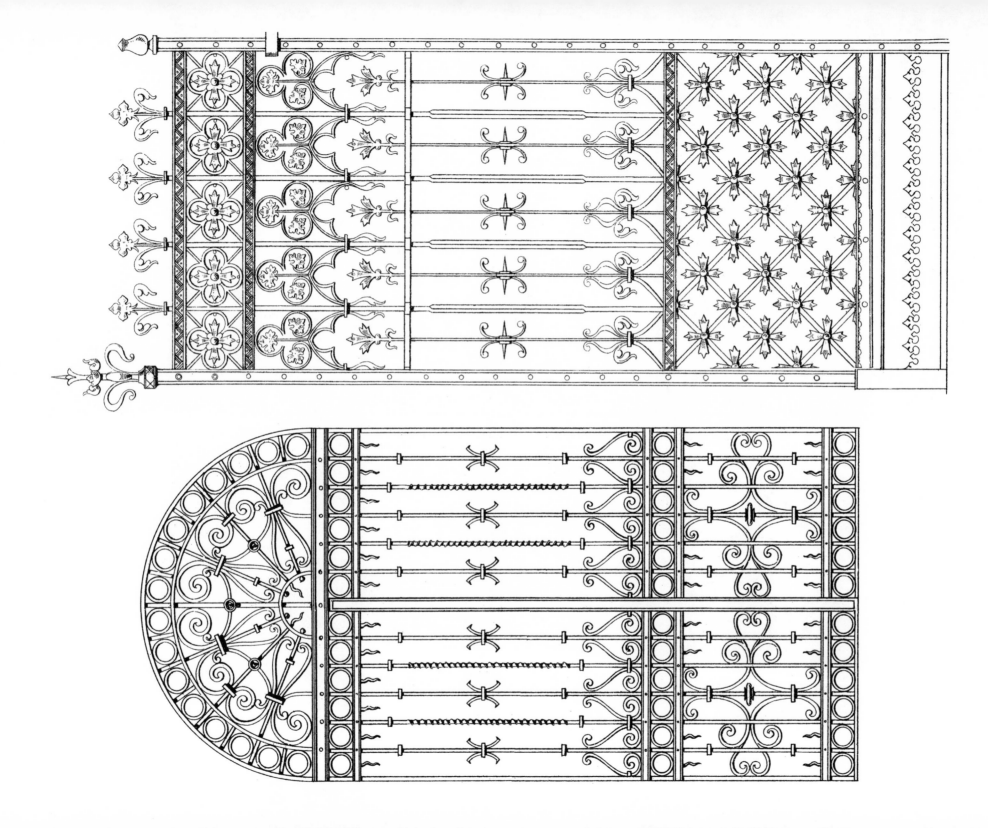

54   Door, gate

Entry gate   55

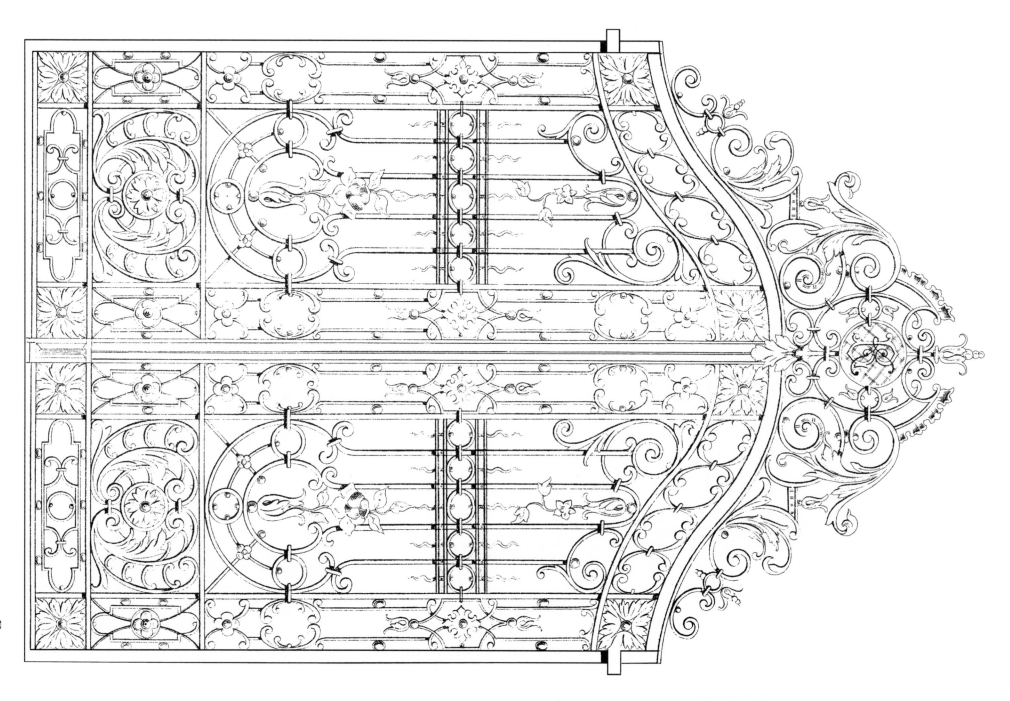

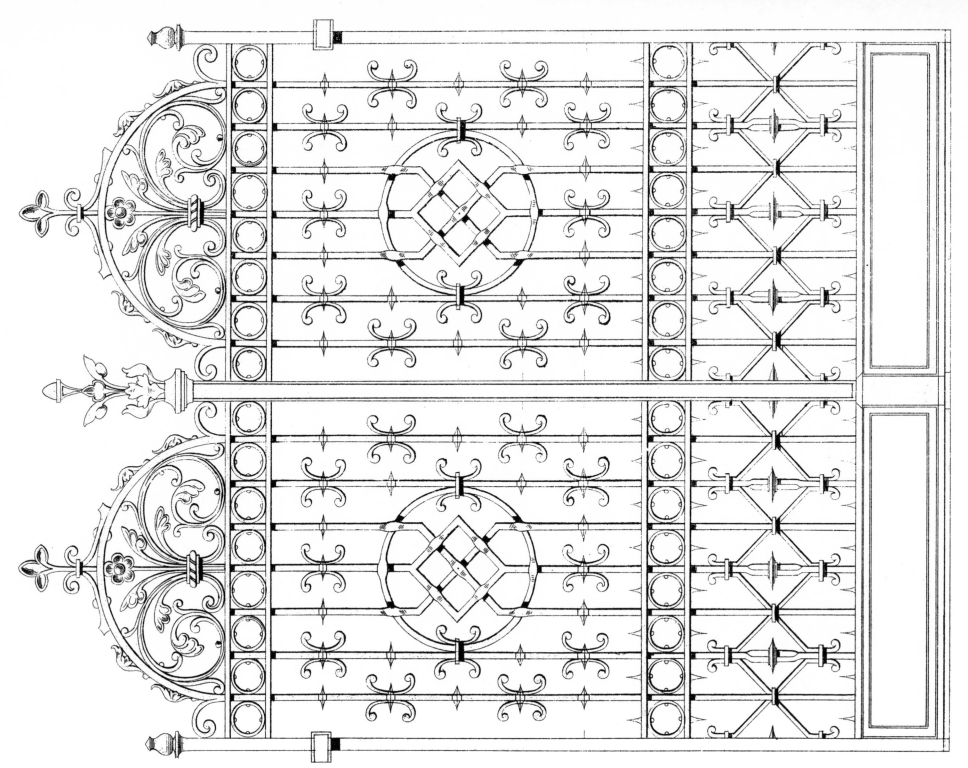

58 Gate

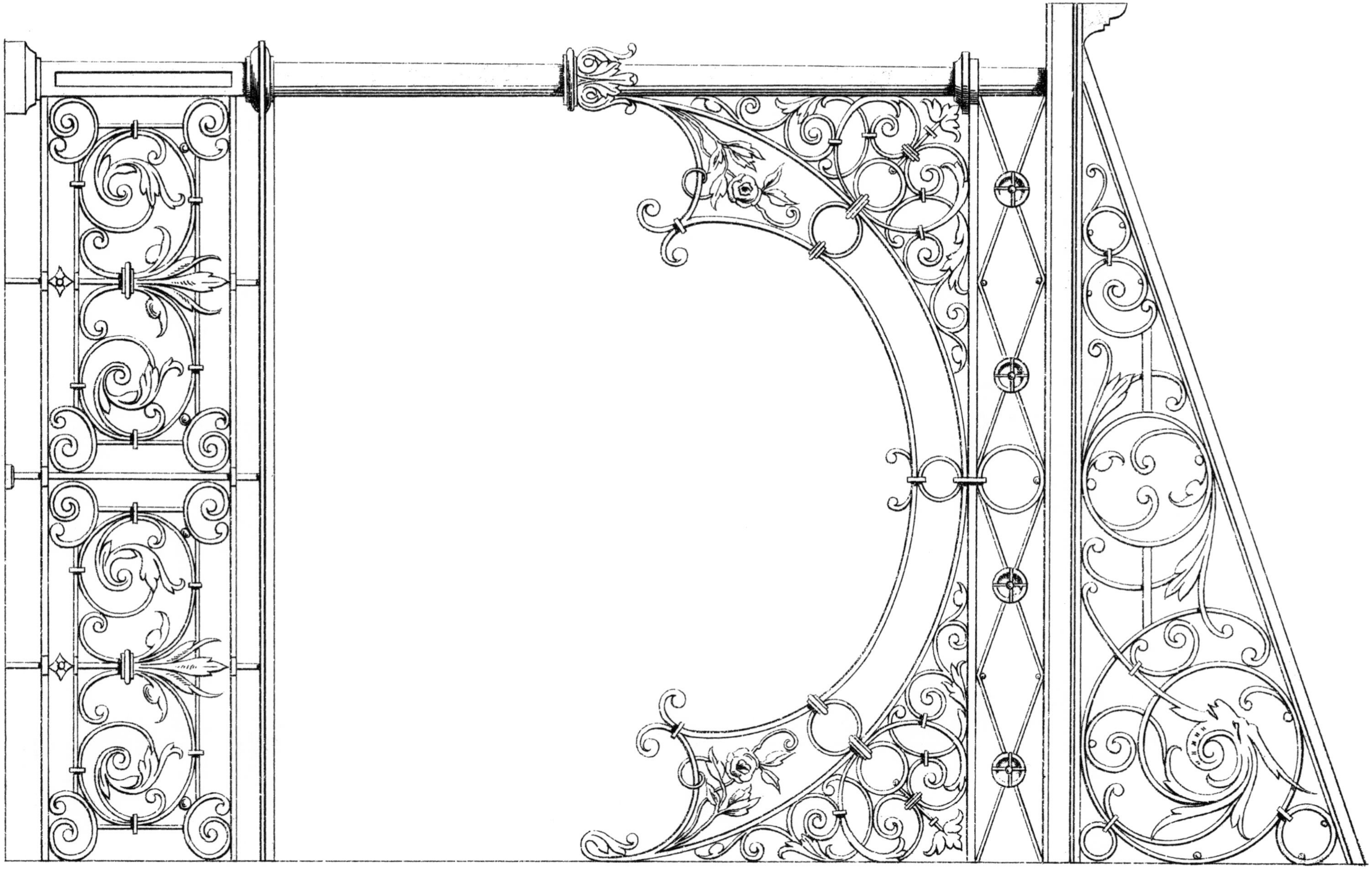

Veranda 59

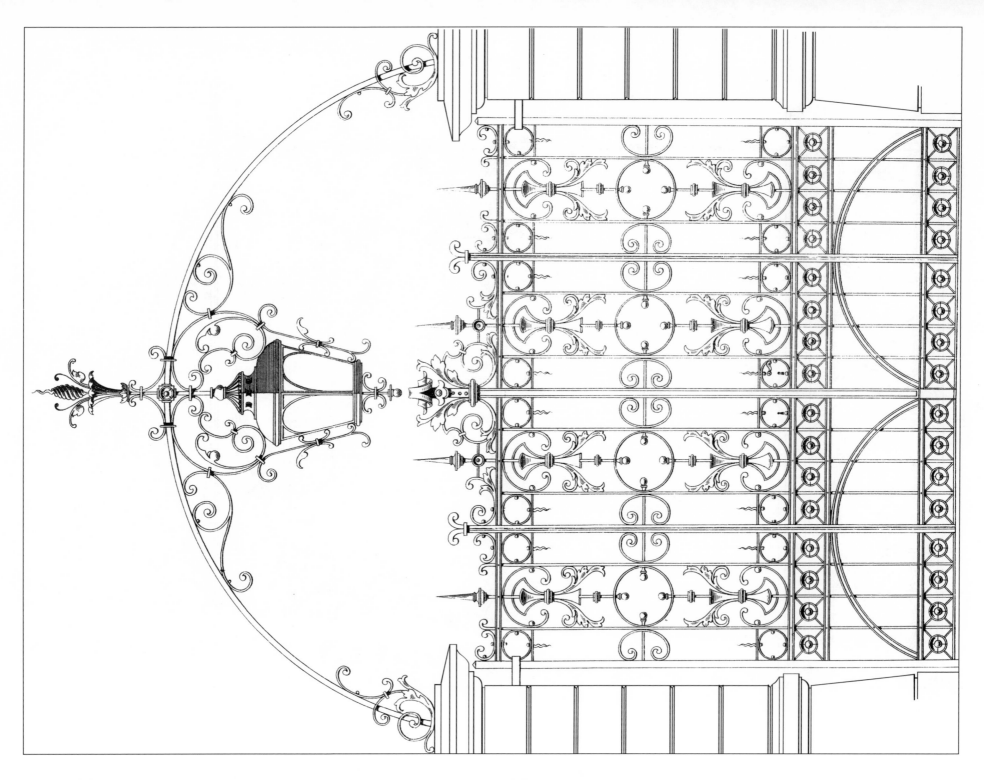

60　Entry gate

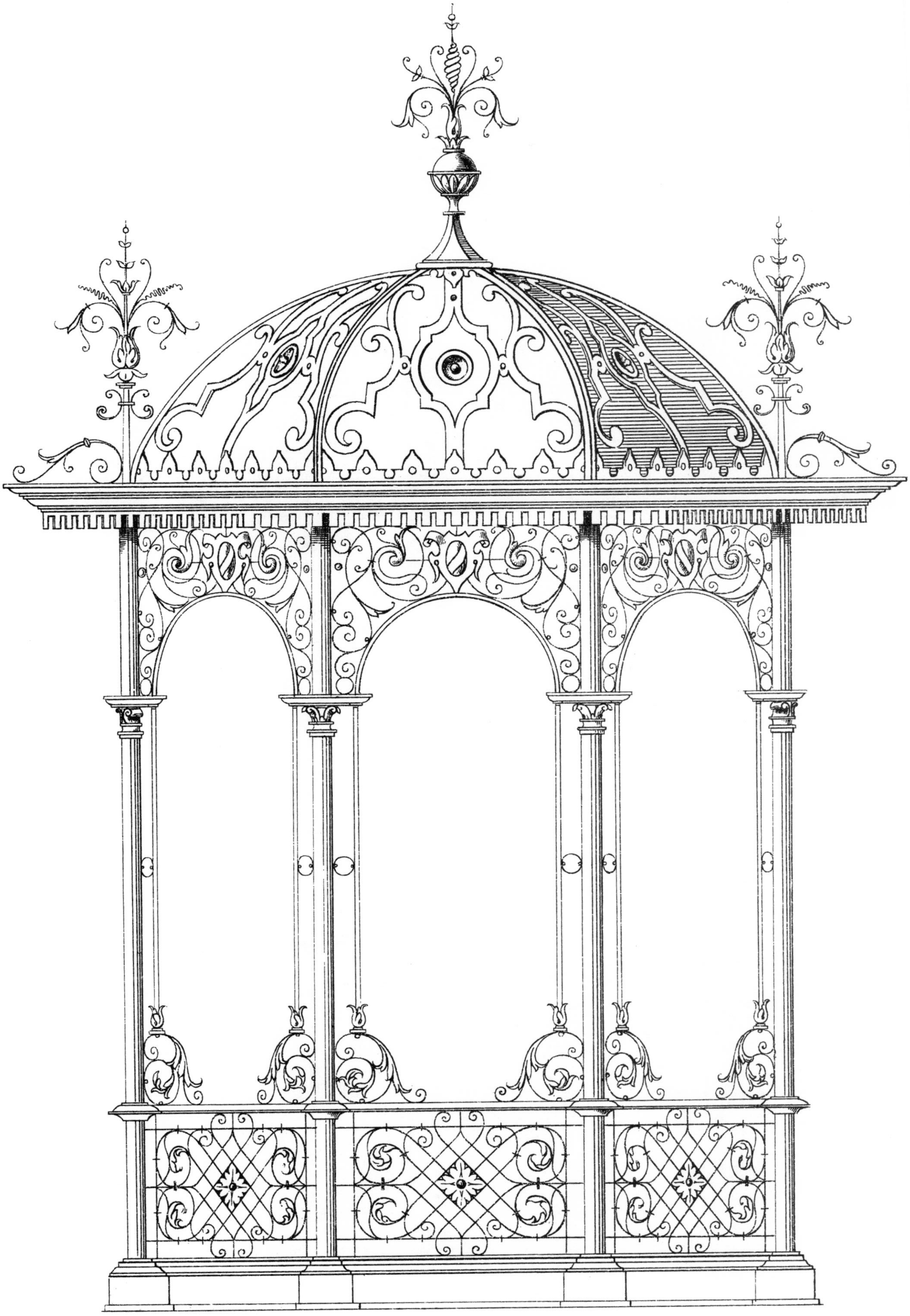

Veranda garden house *61*

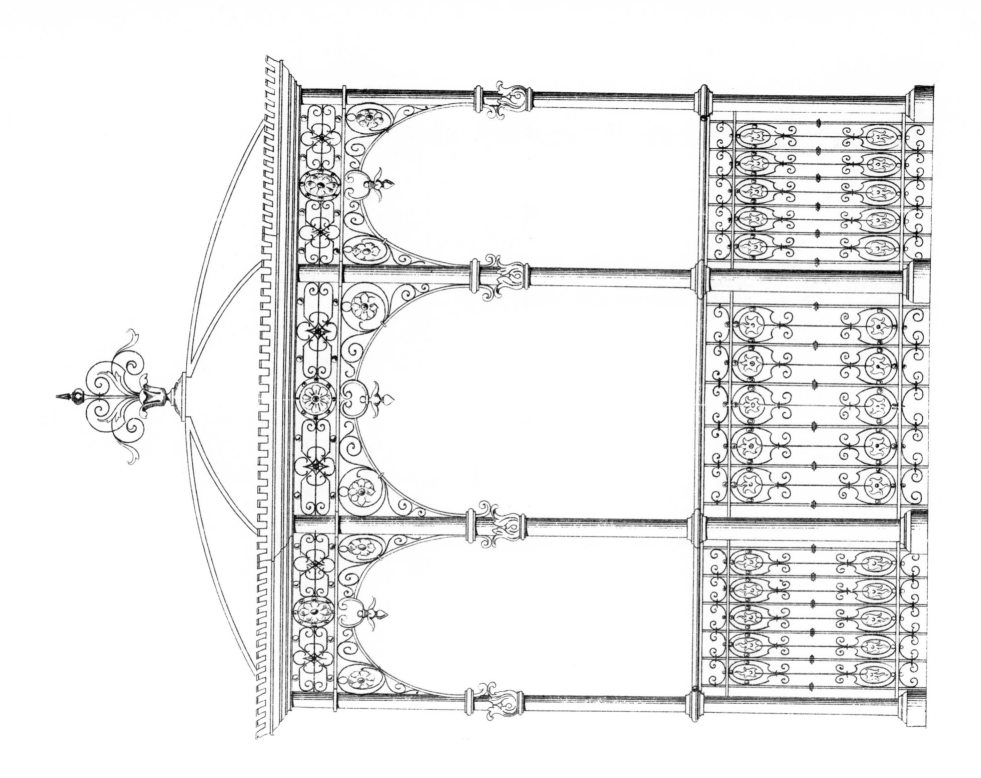

62   Veranda garden house

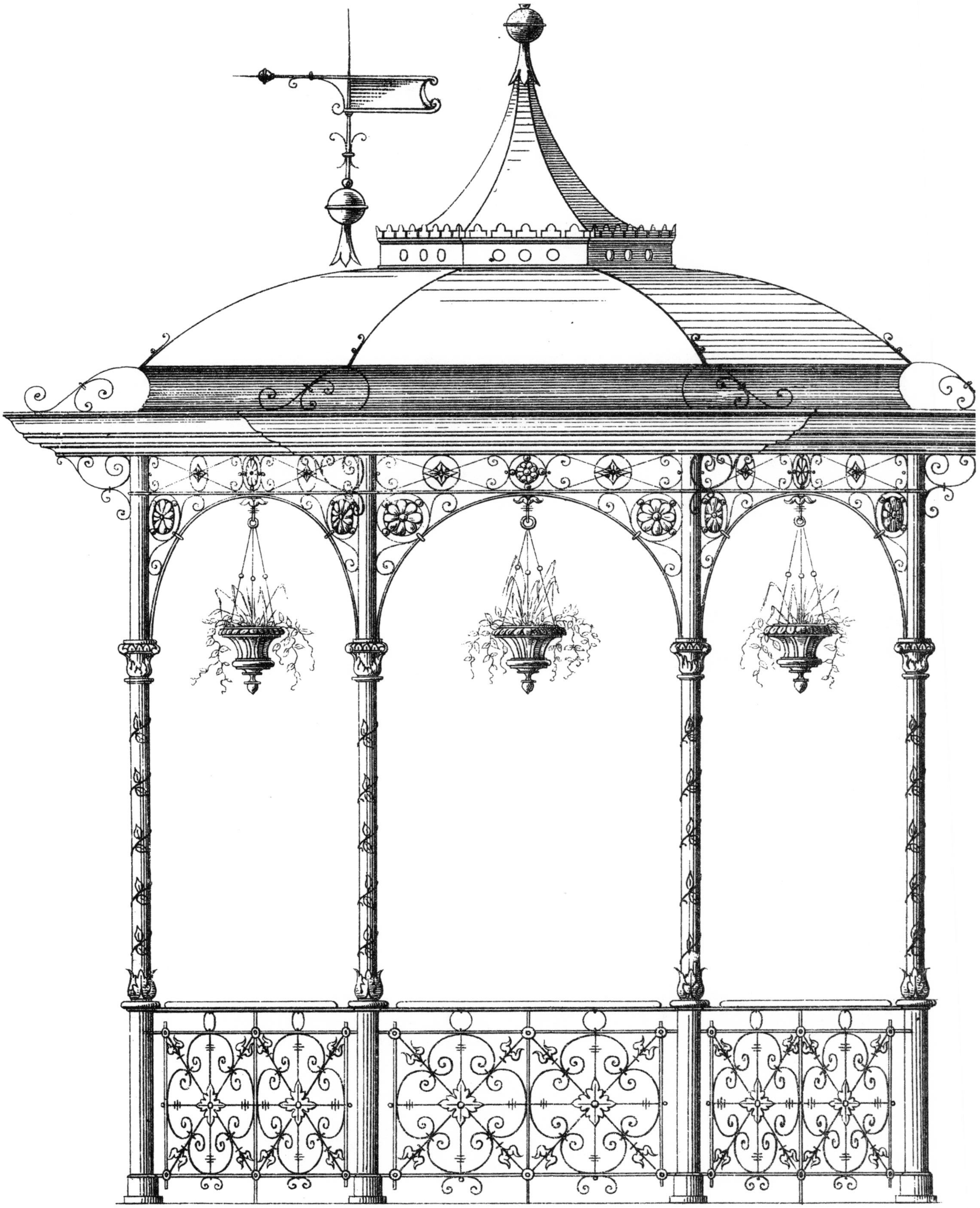

Veranda garden house

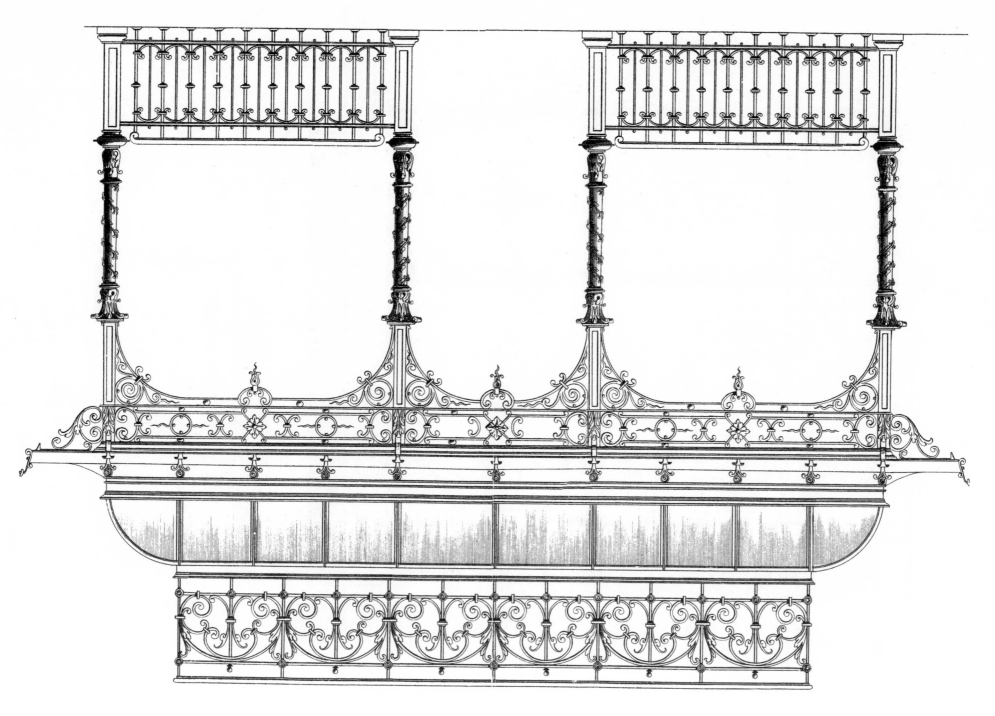

Veranda

Veranda 65

66   Veranda with corrugated tin roof

CONCERT- HALLE.

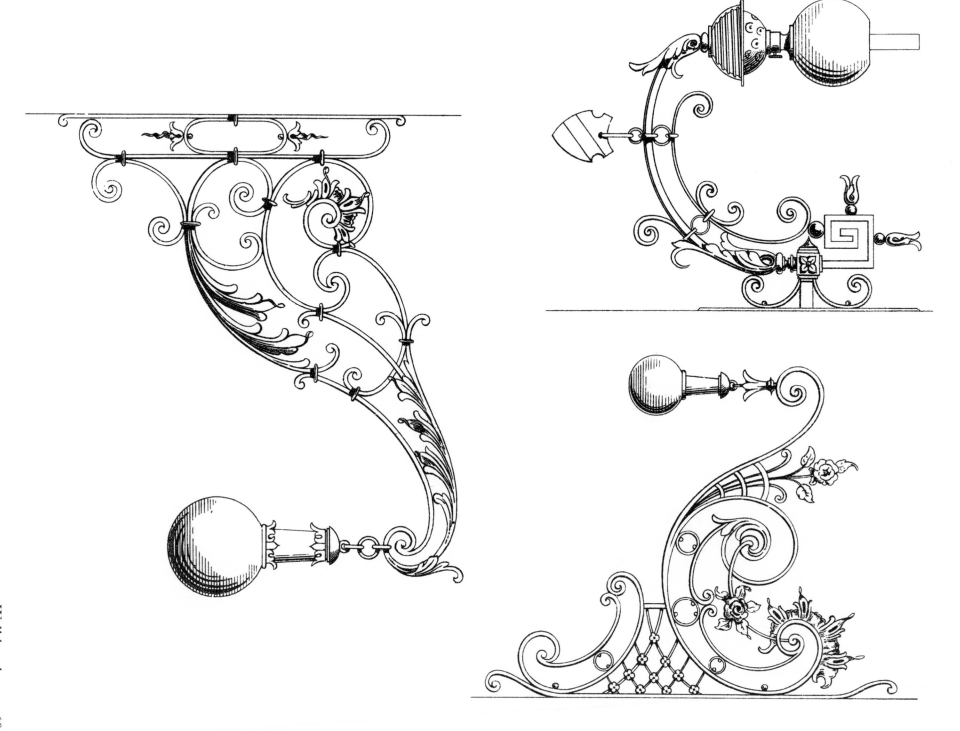

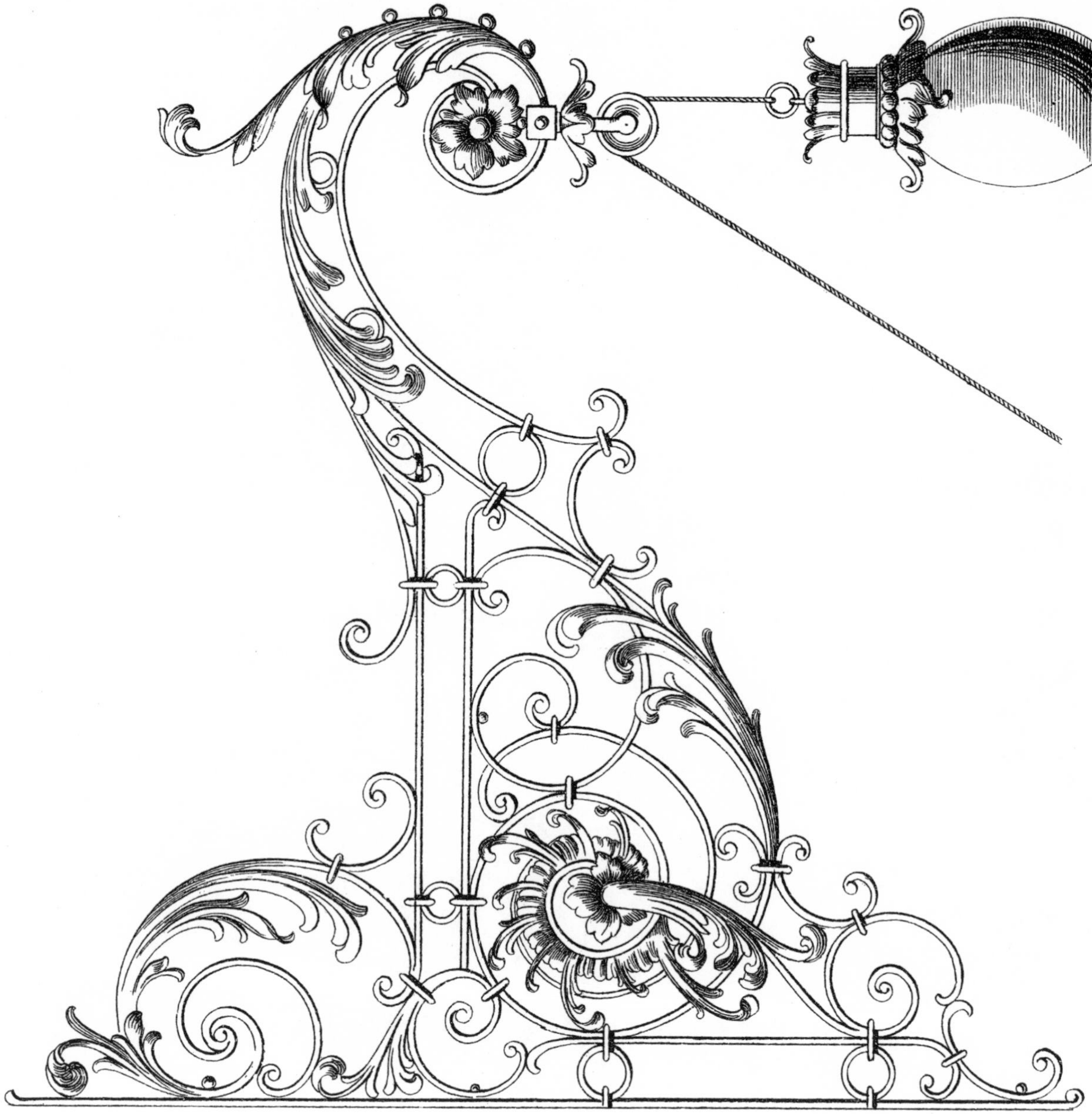

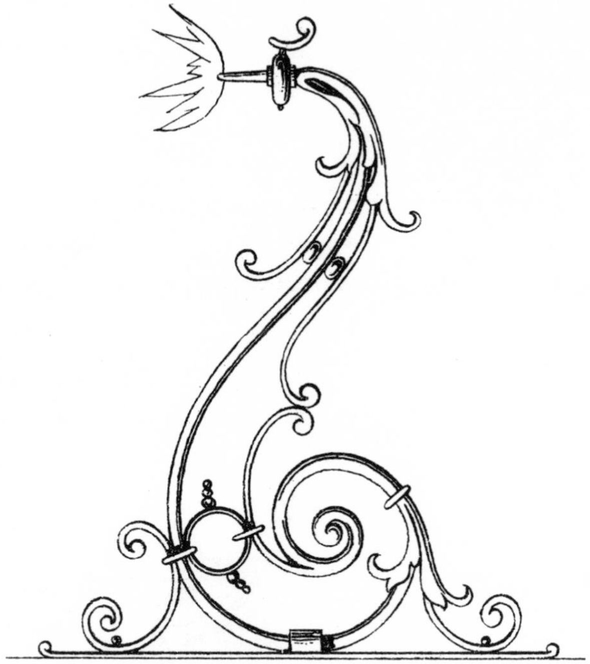

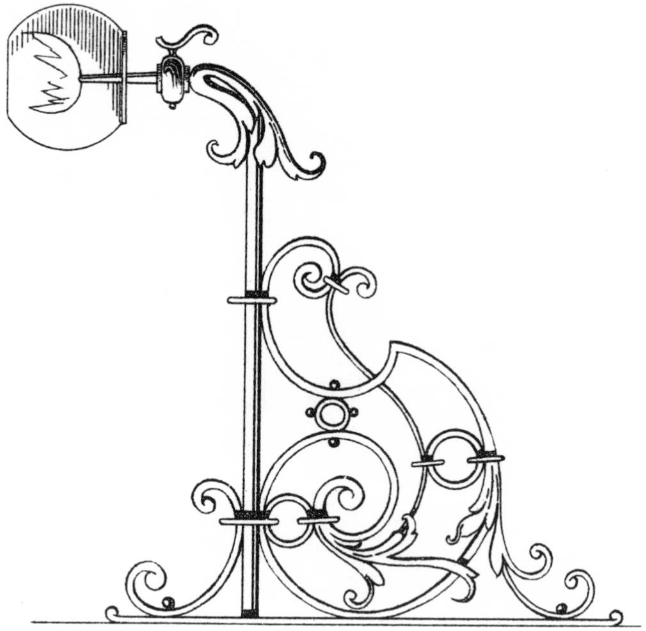

Wall brackets

72 Wall brackets, light stand

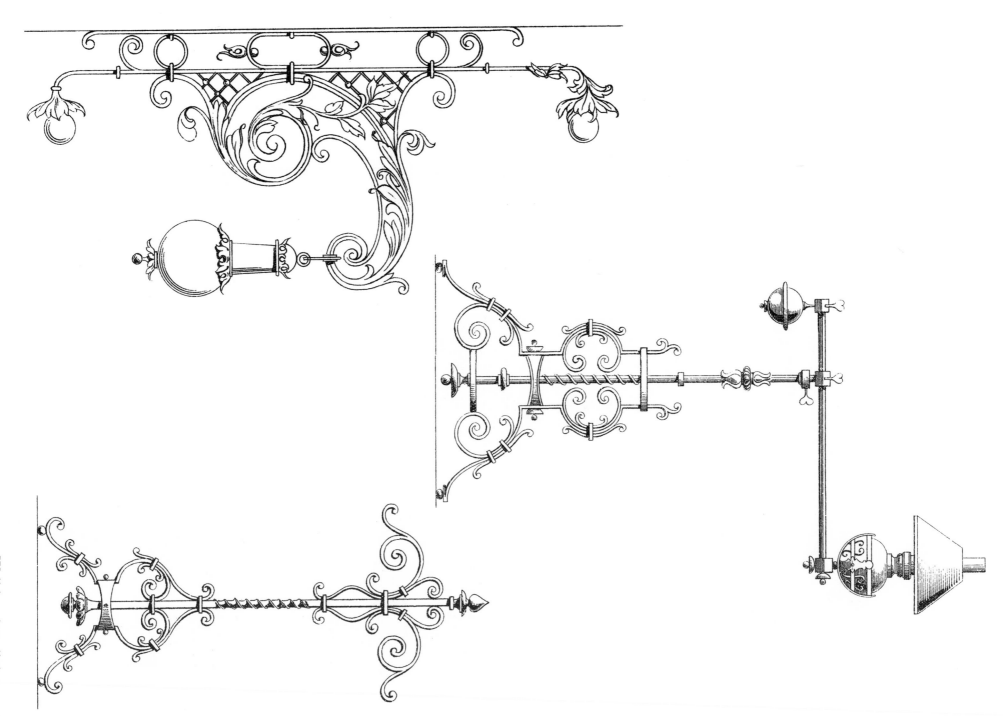

74   Light stands

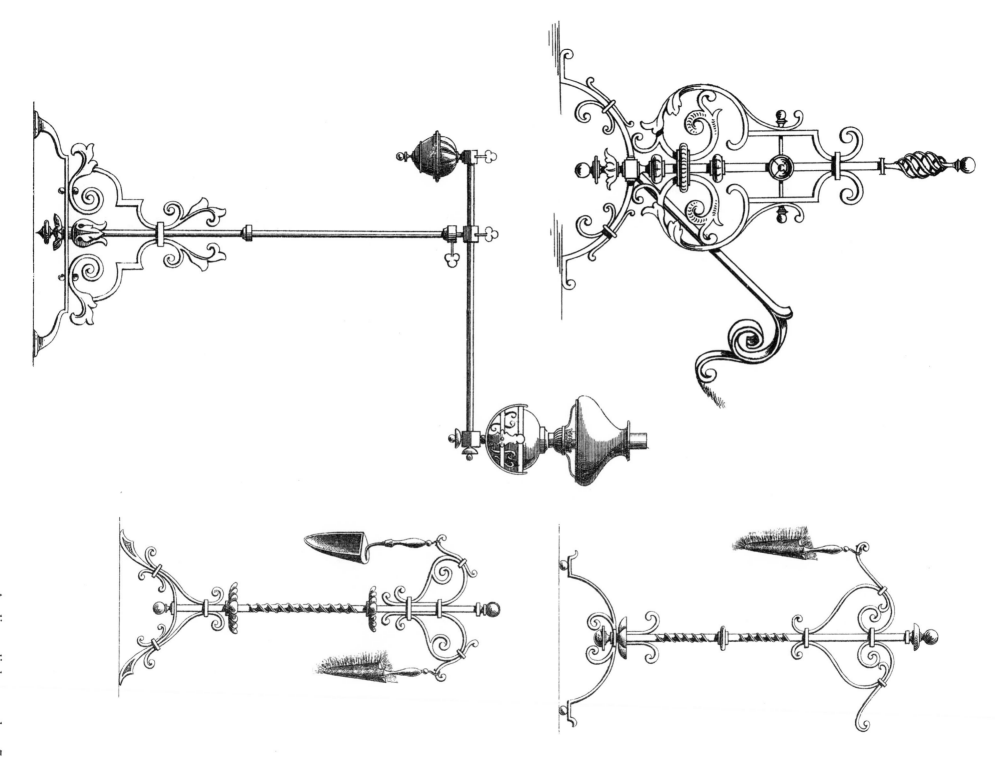

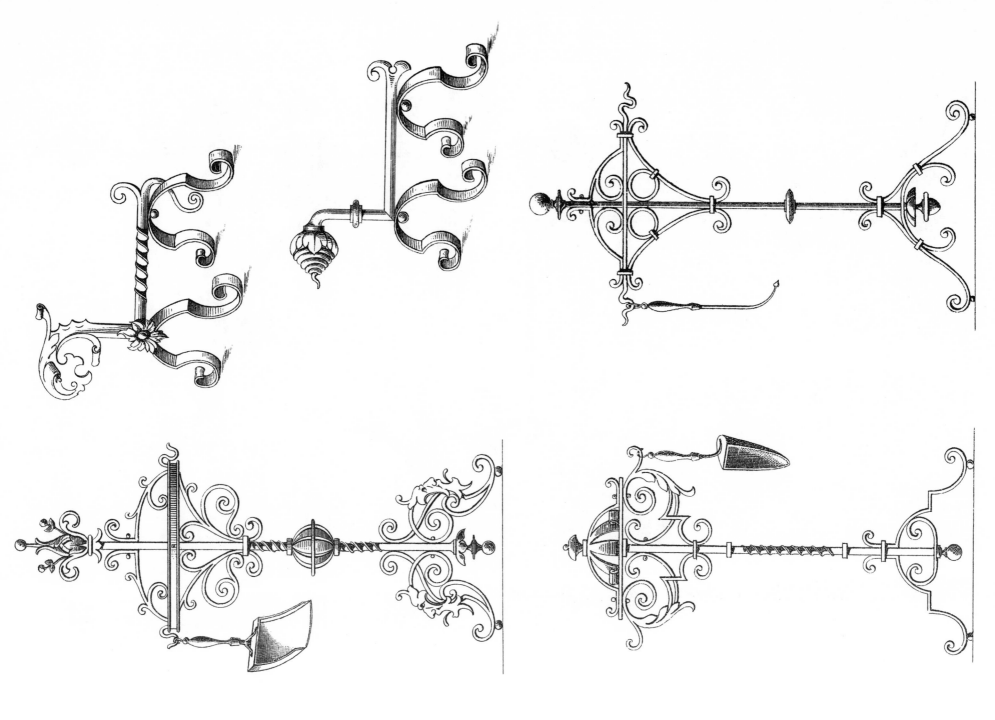

76 Andirons, light stands

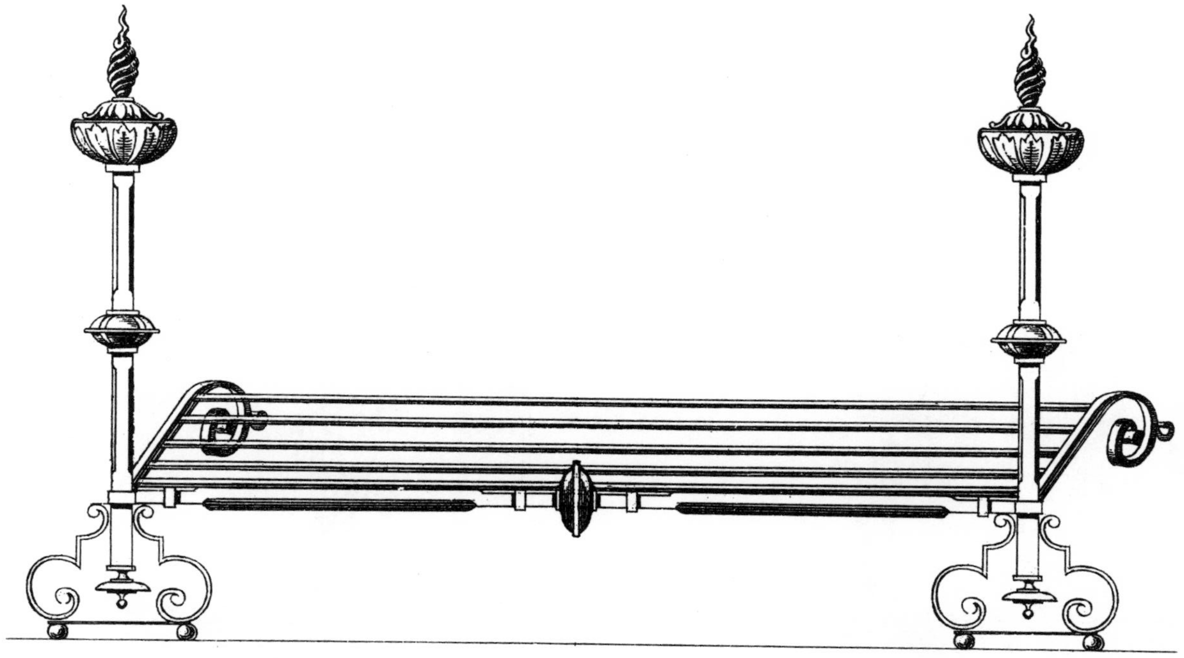

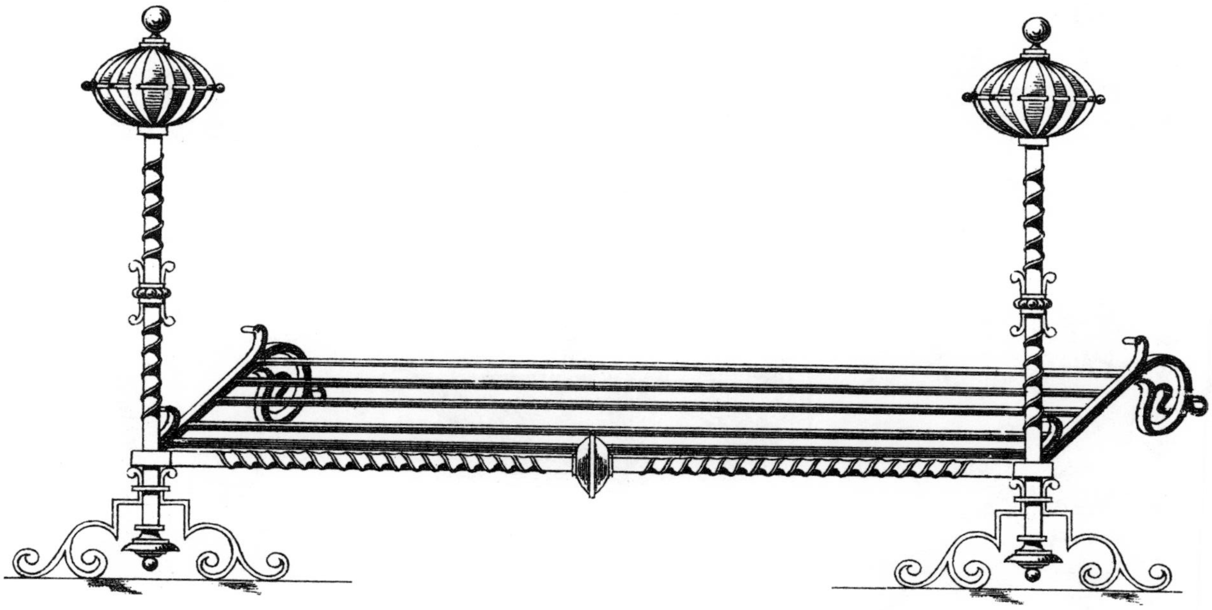

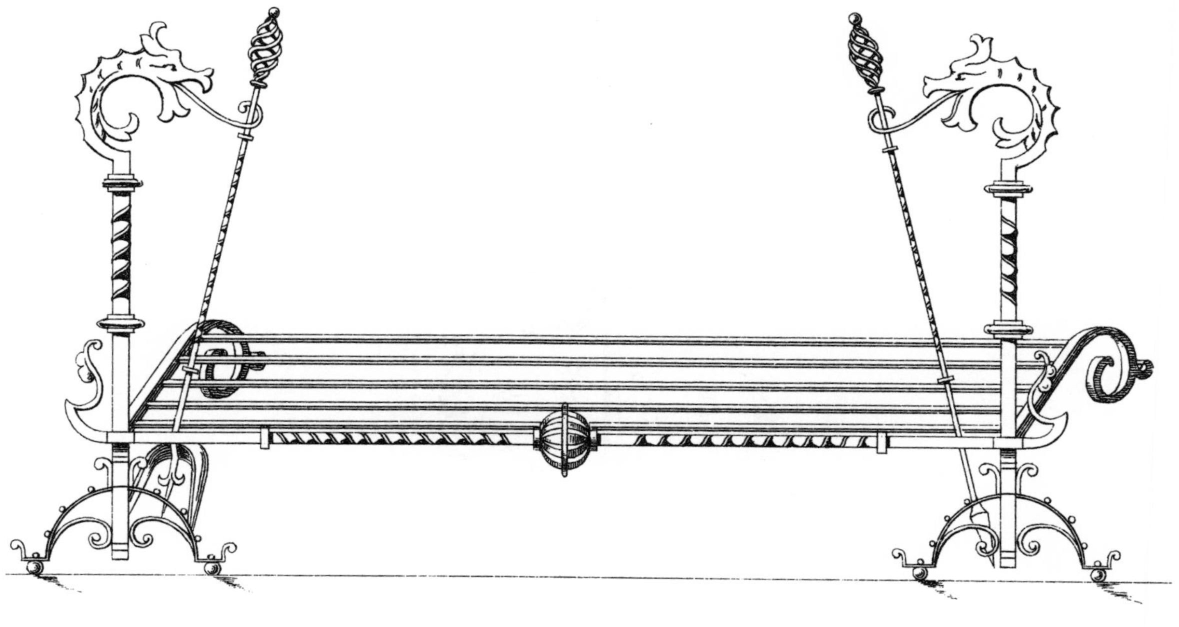

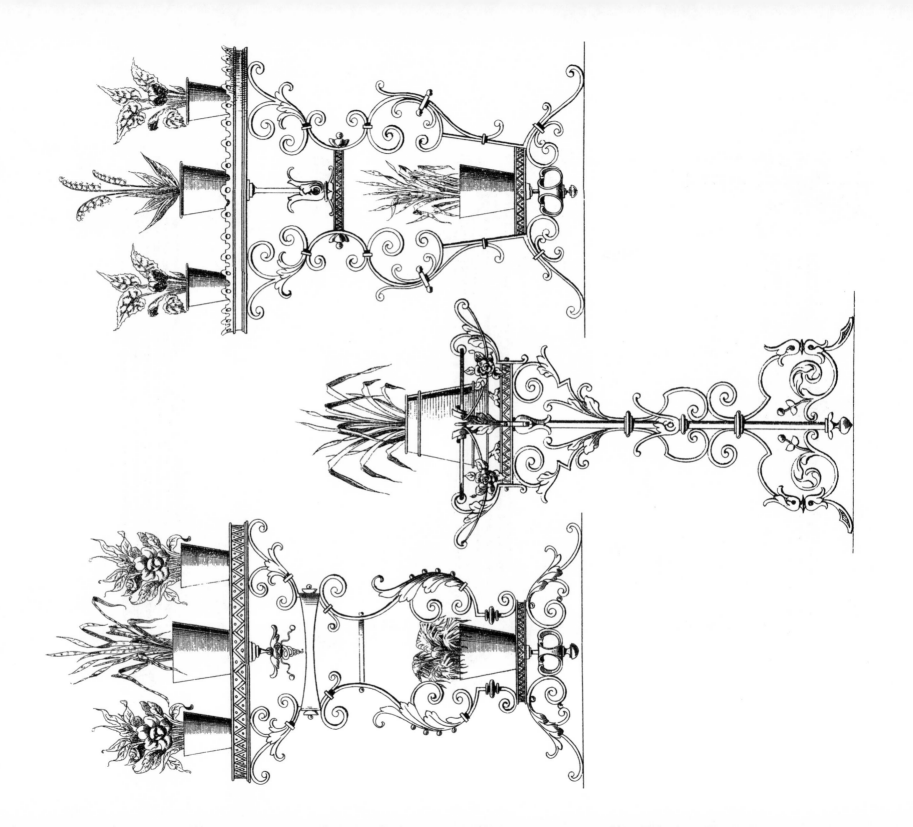

78 Flower stands

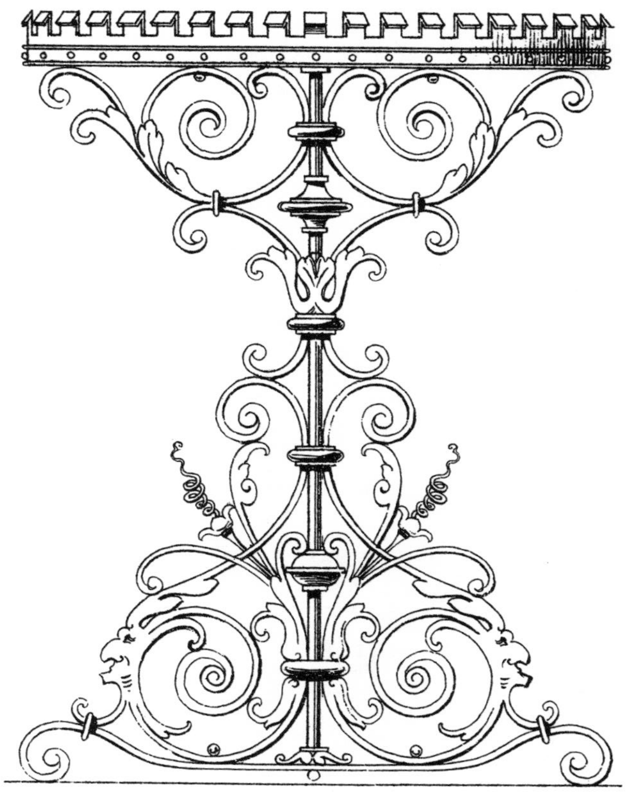

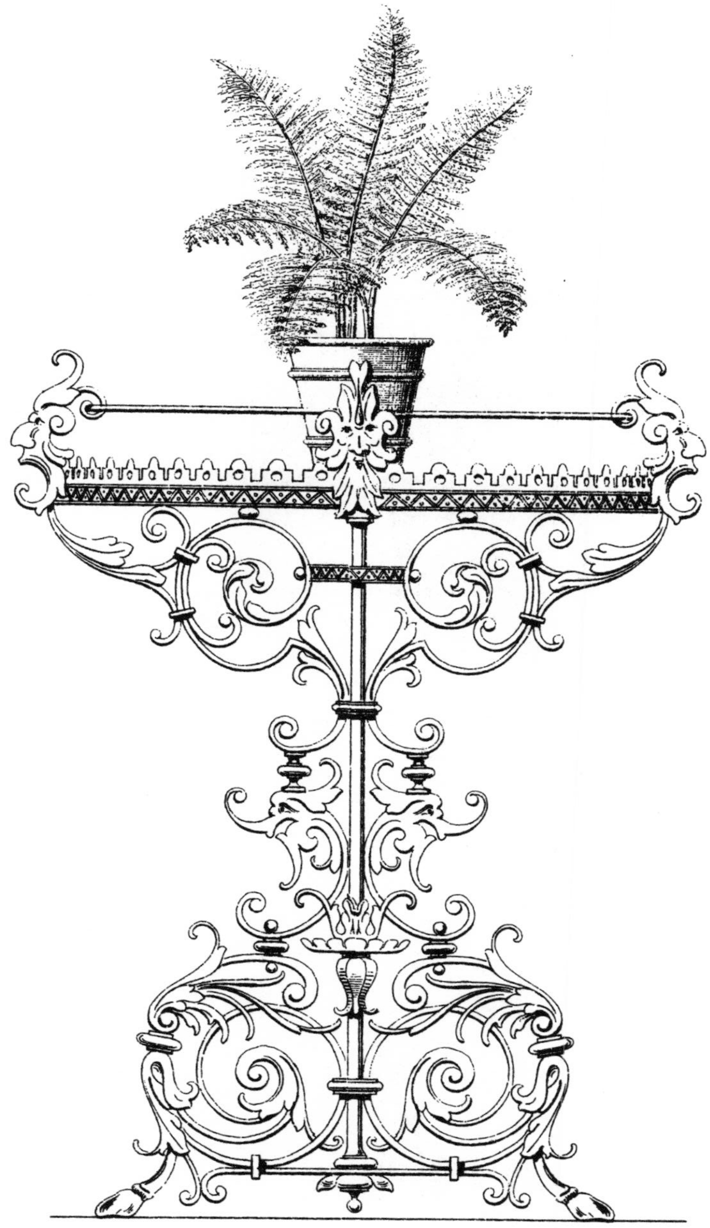

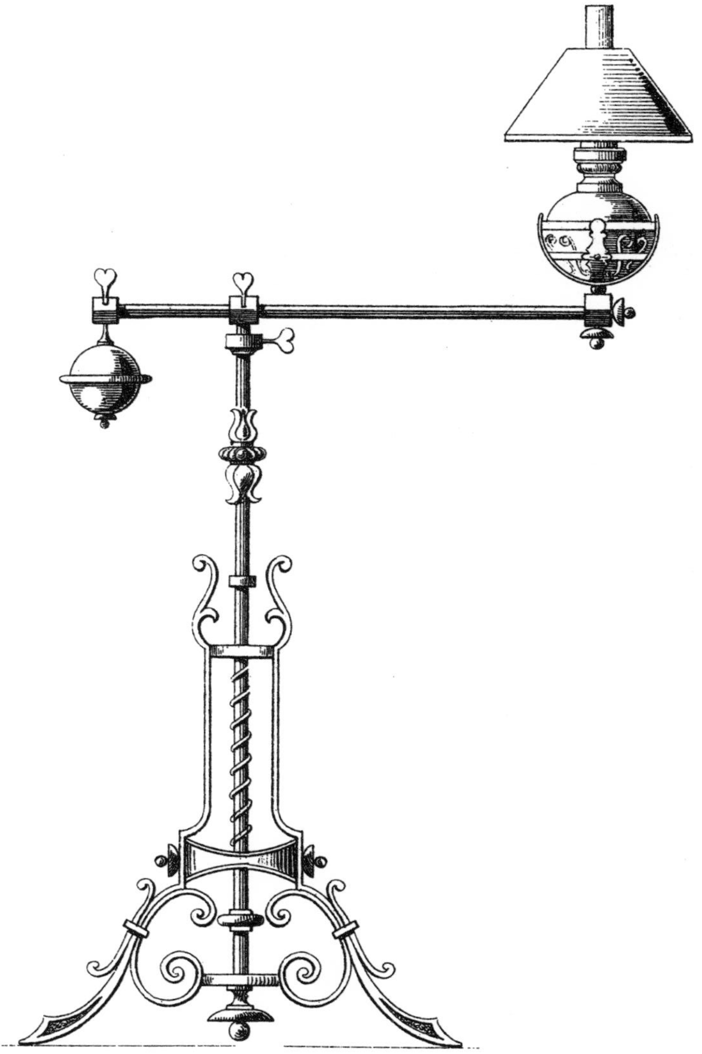

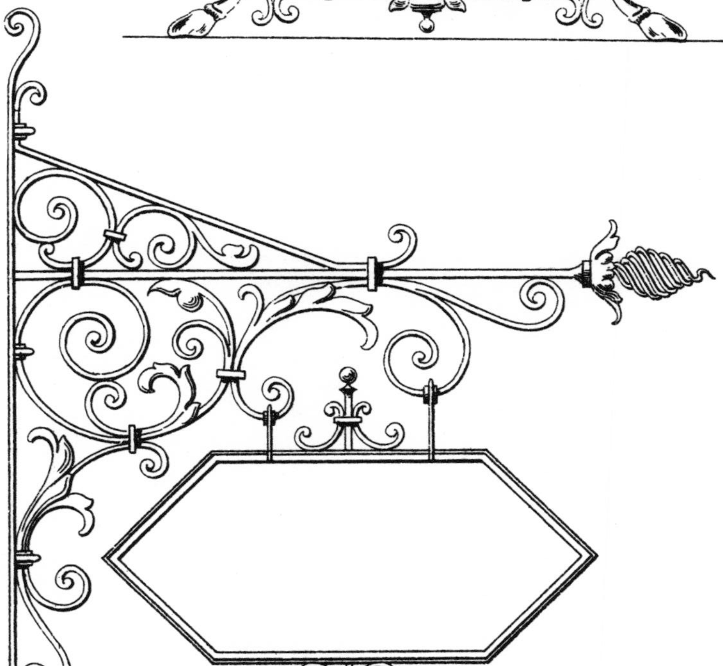

Flower stands, light stand, commercial sign

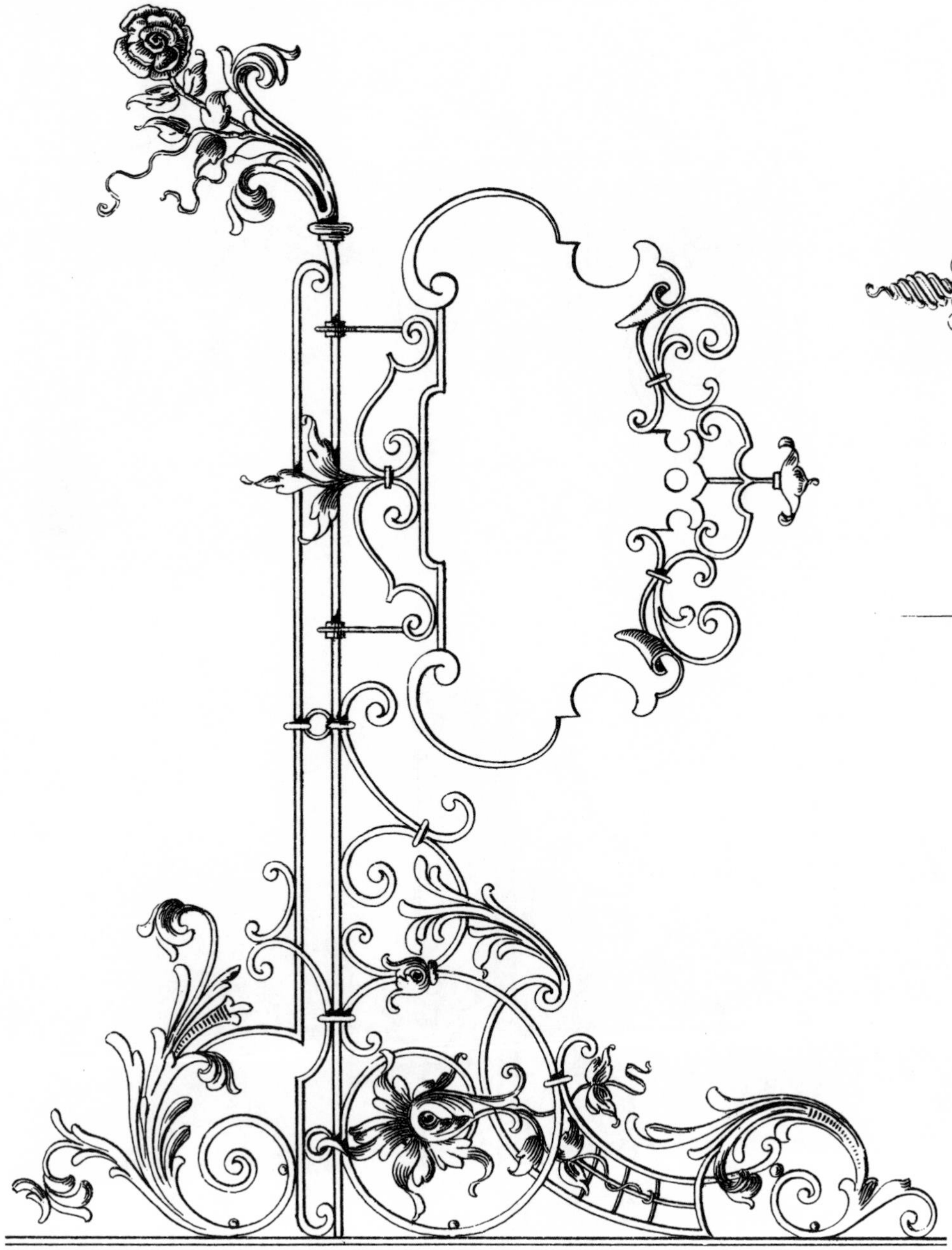

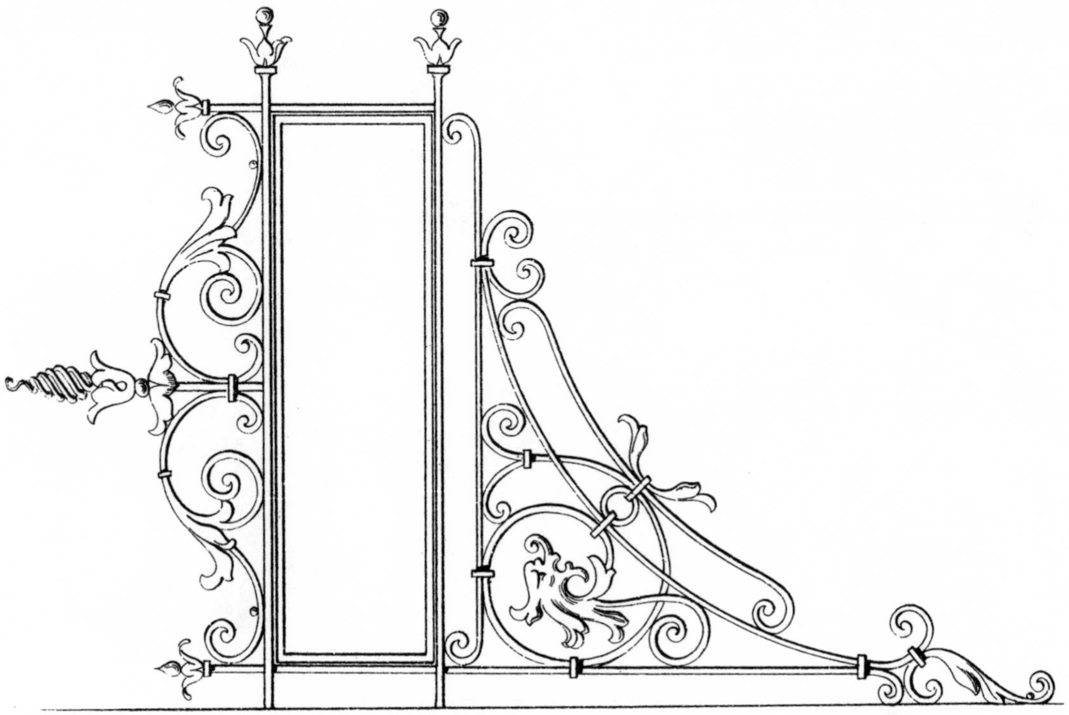

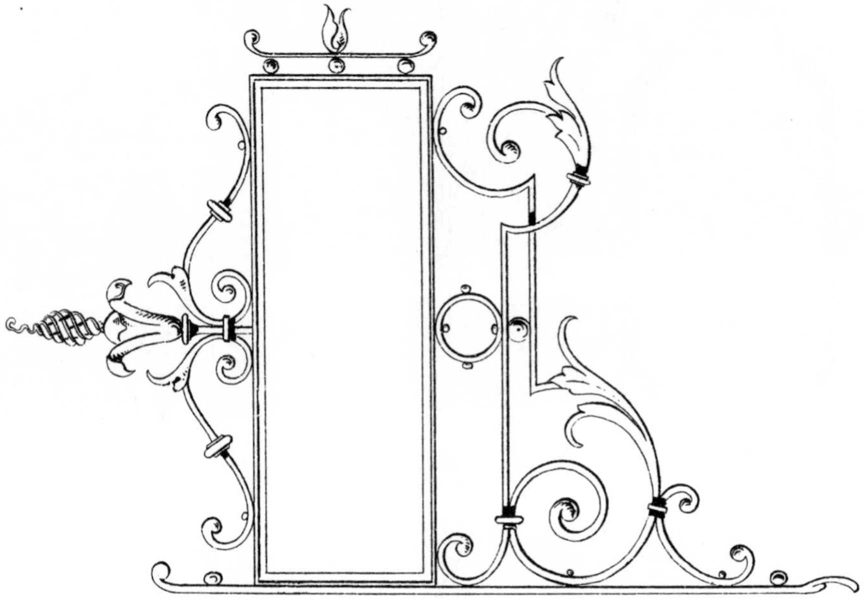

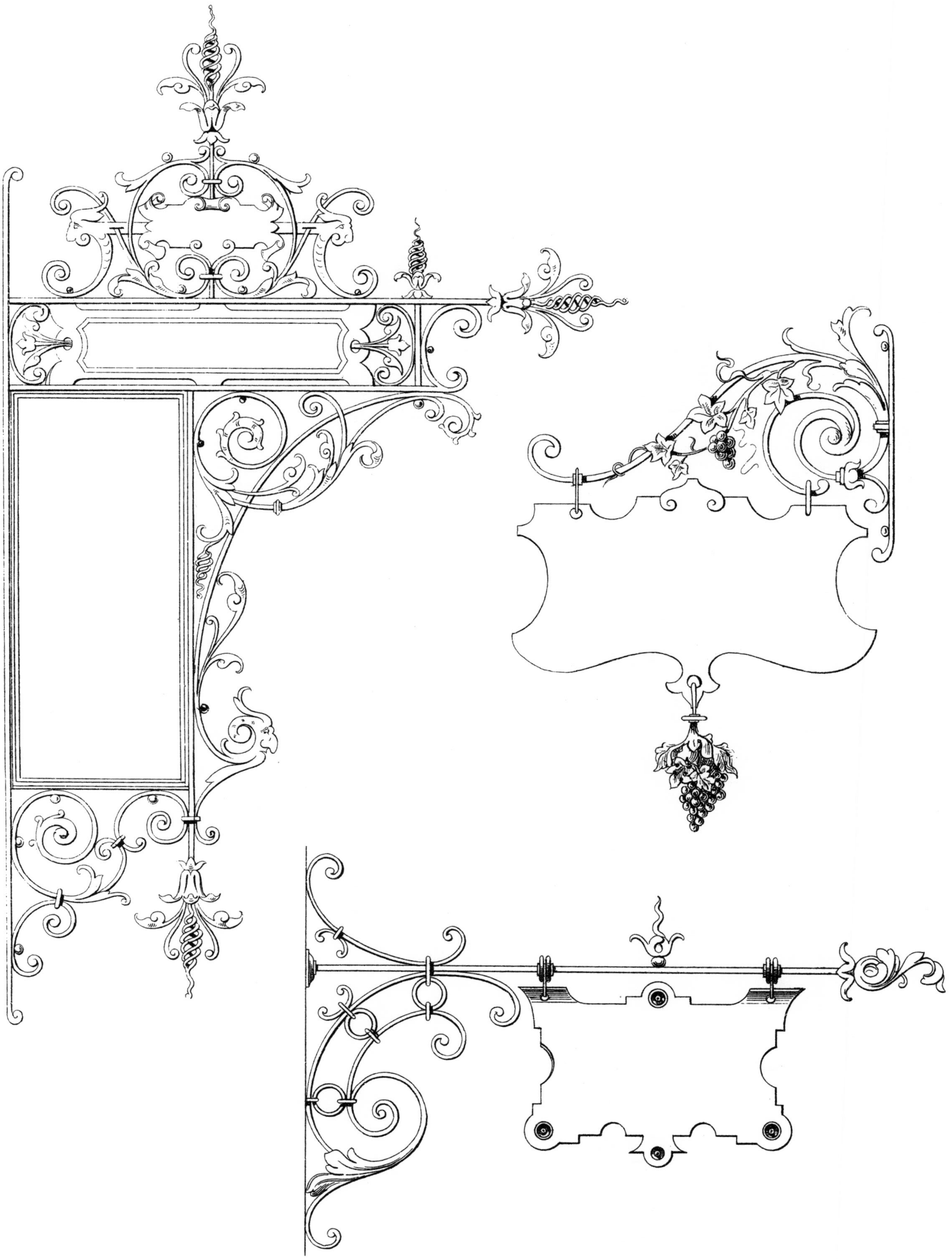

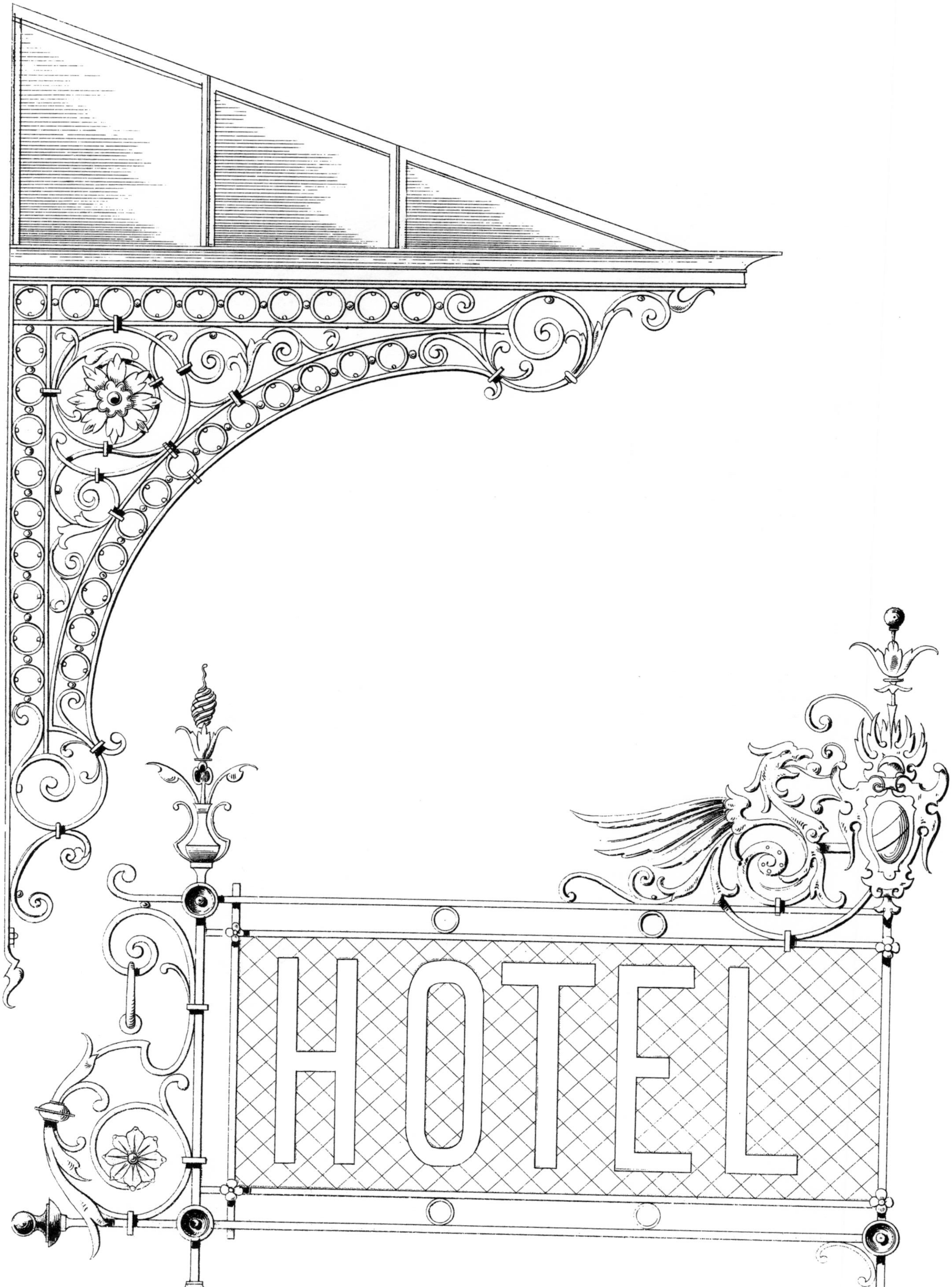

Canopy, commercial sign

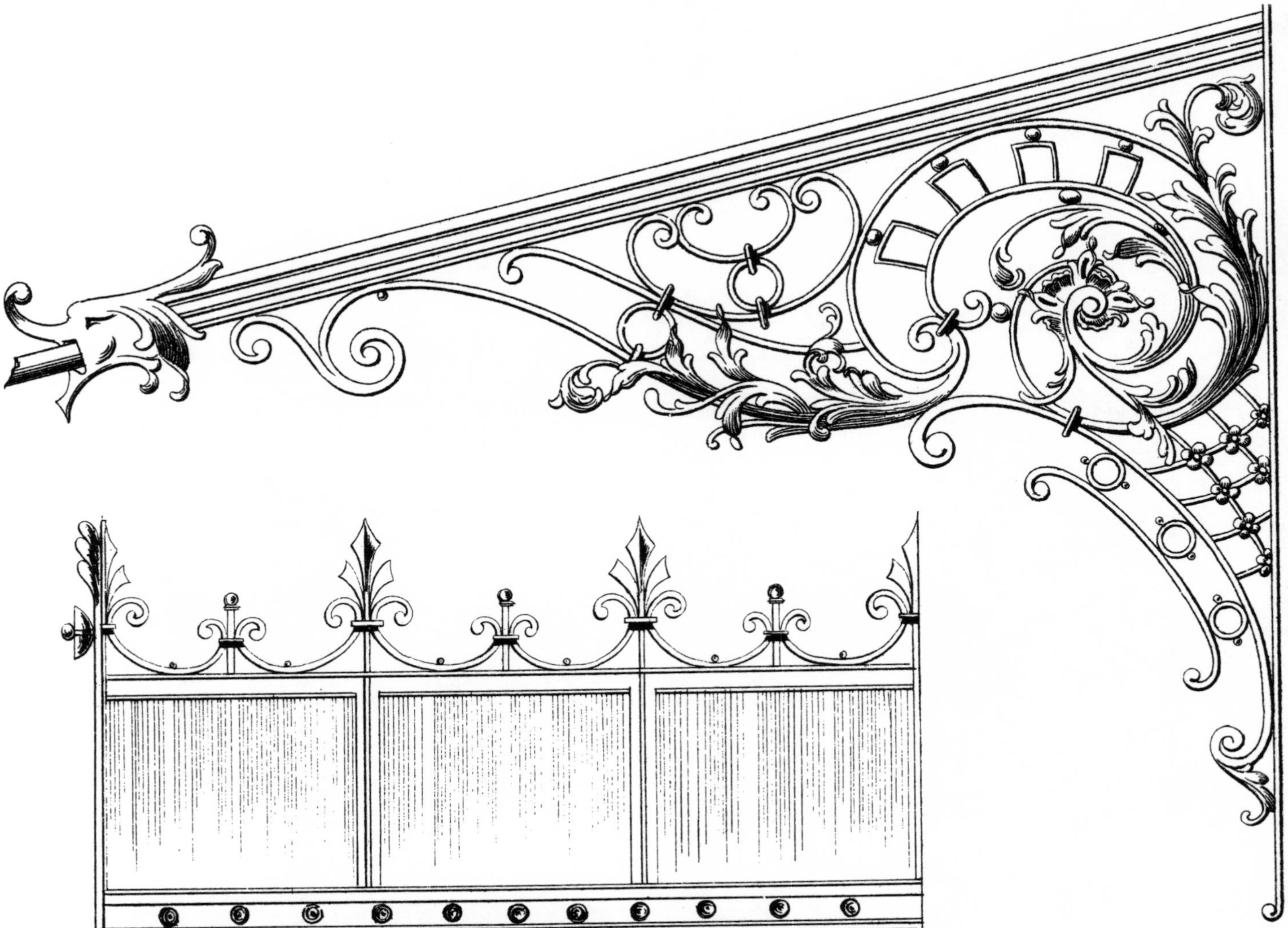

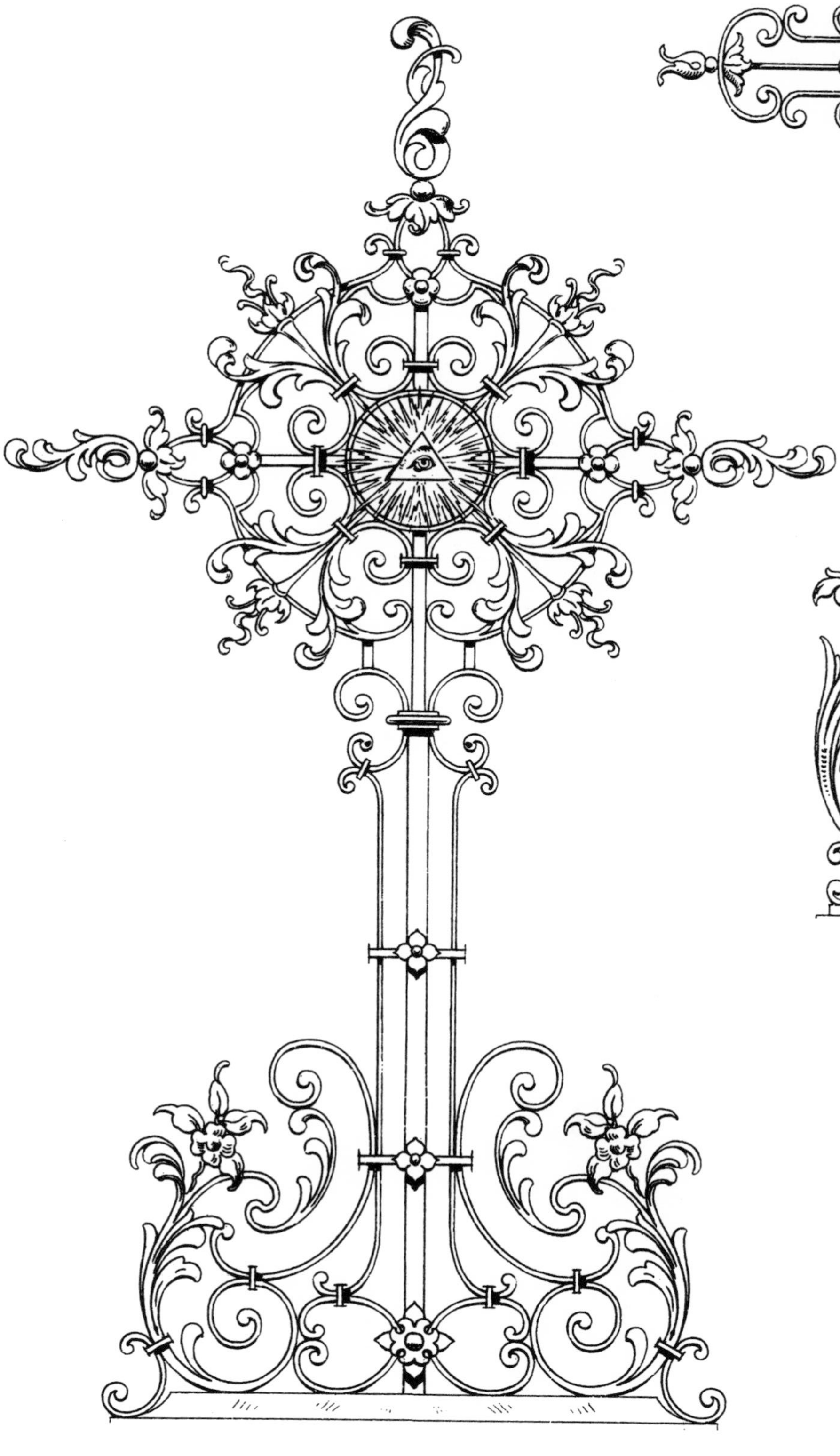
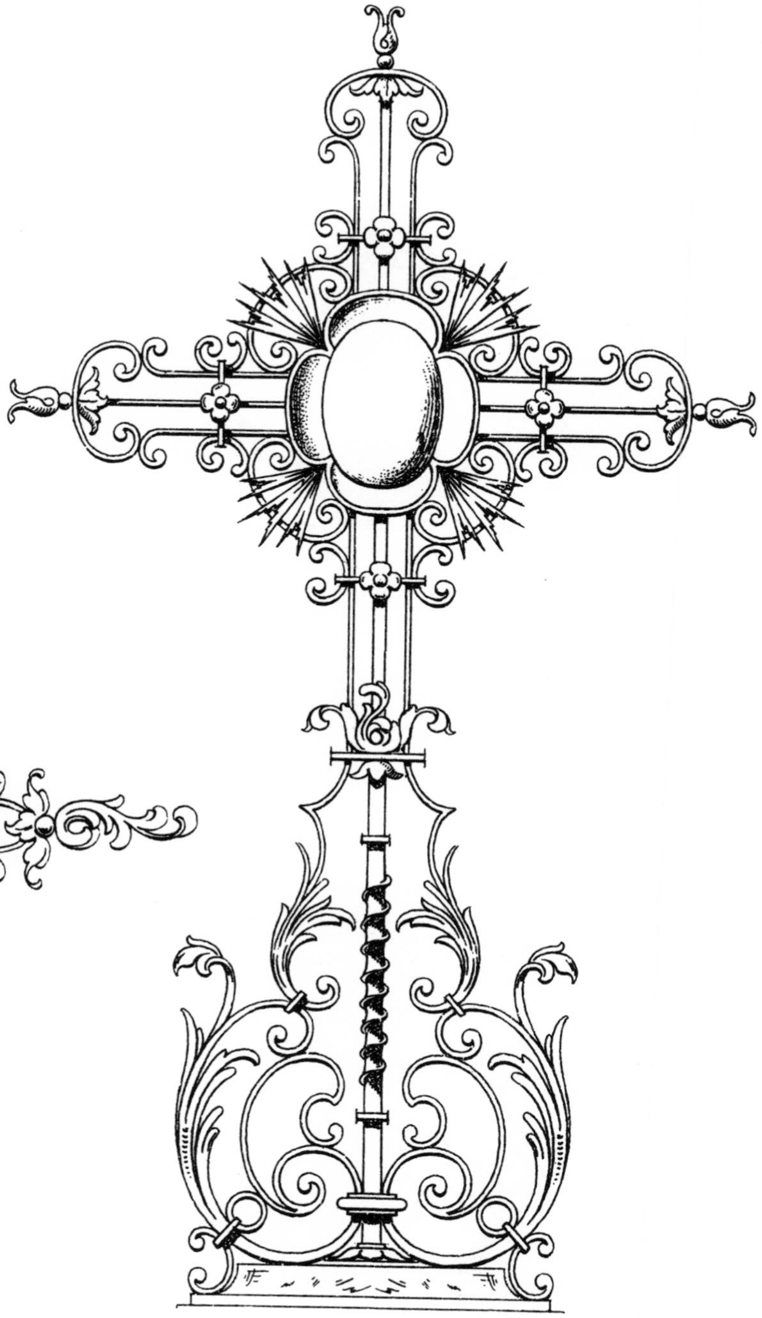

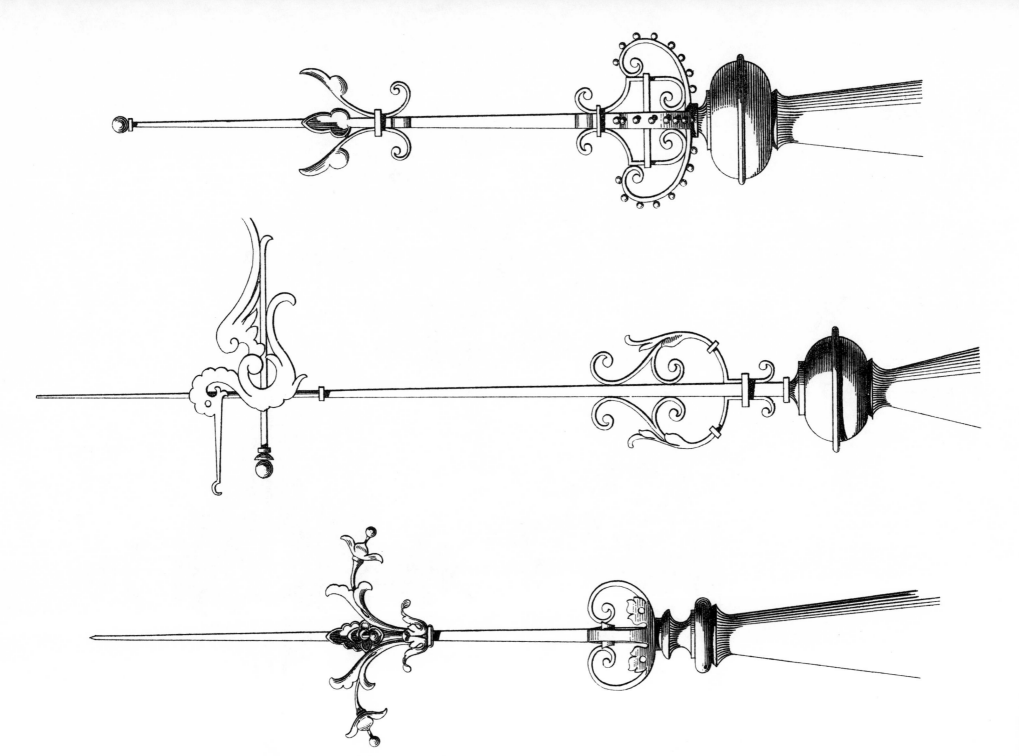

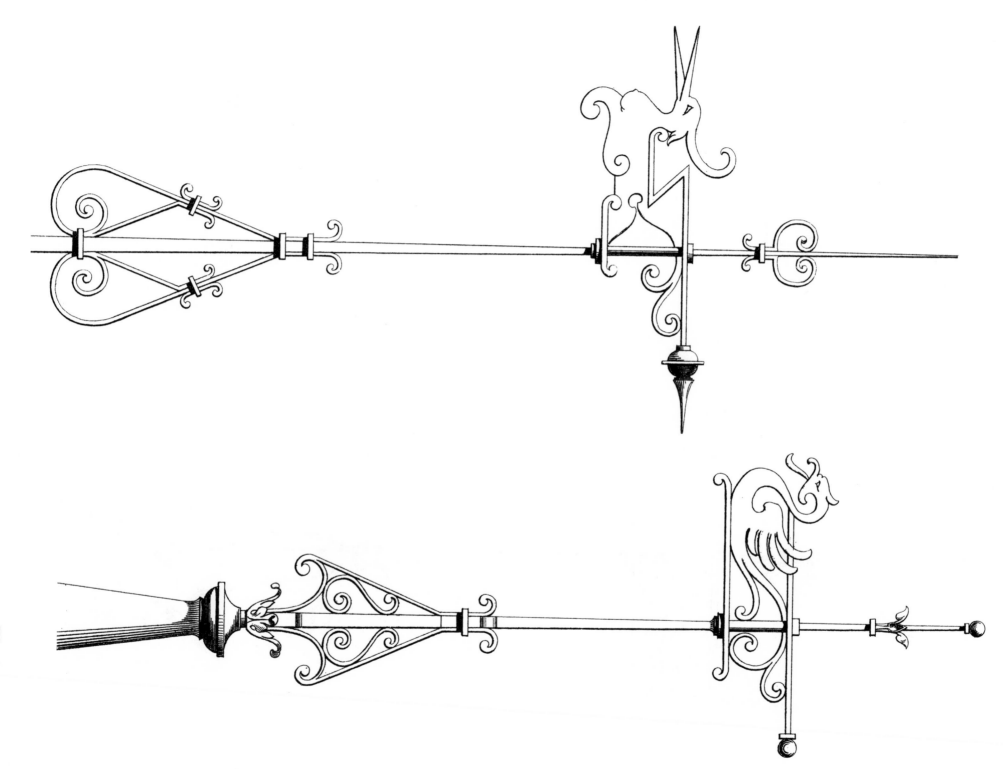

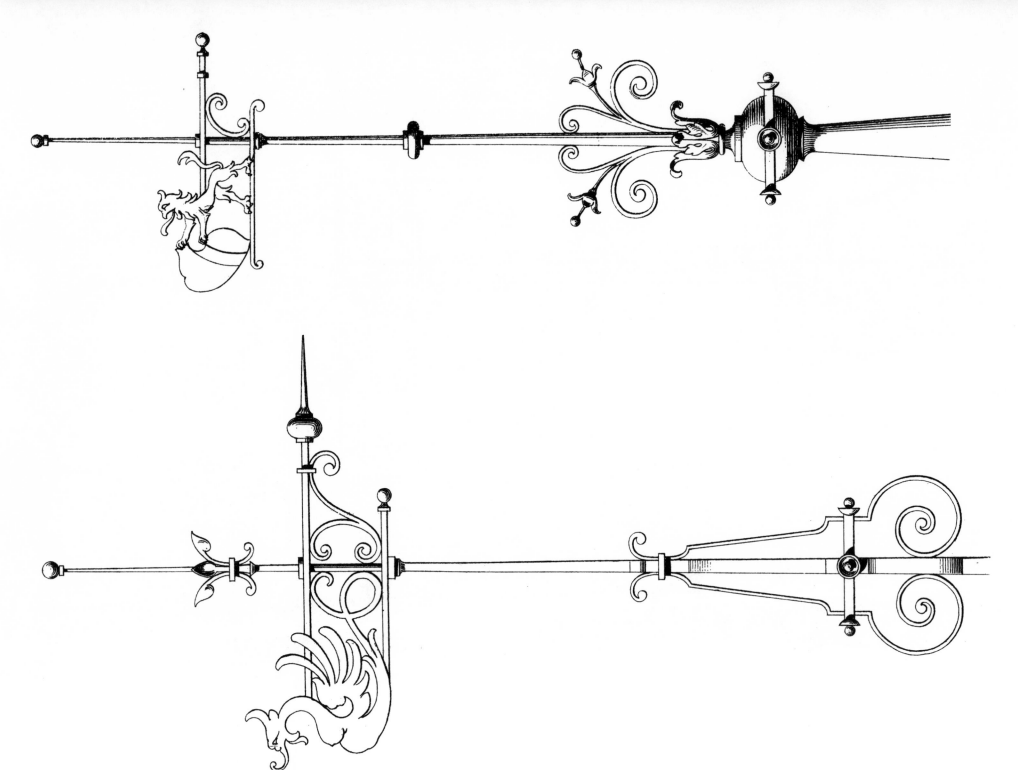

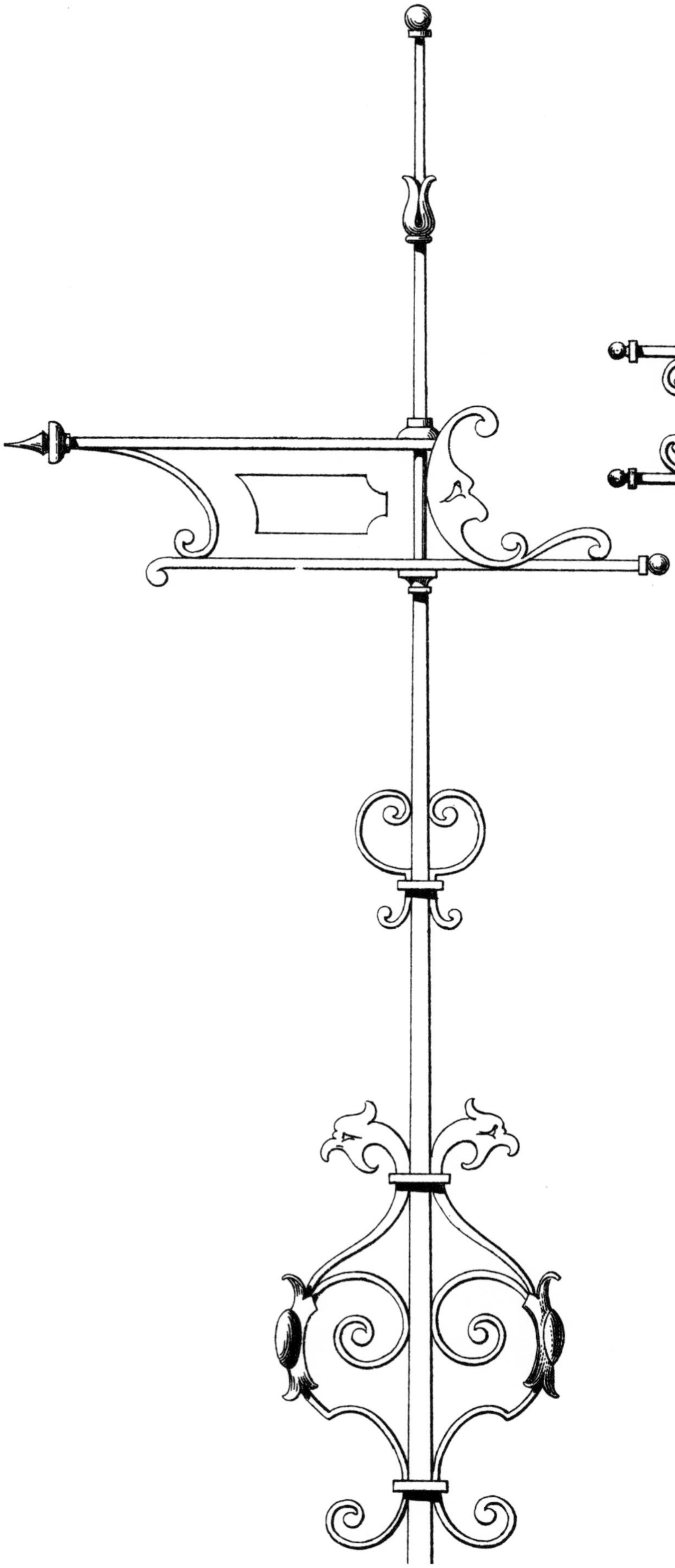

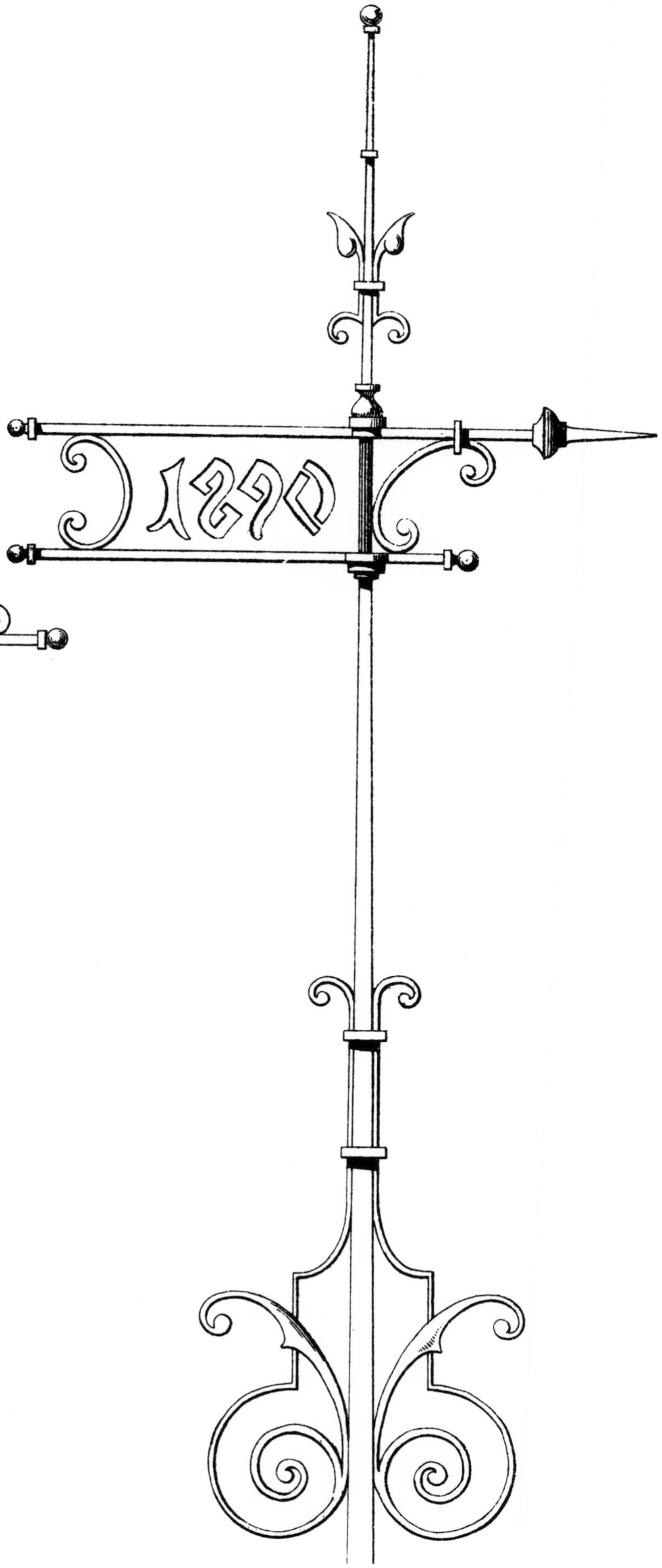